How To Sell Your Business

Kaloian Kirilov

ISBN 978-93-5610-681-9

Published in India 2022 by Pencil

Contributors:

Co-Author: Professor Sanjay Rout
Editor: Professor Prangyan Biswal

A brand of
One Point Six Technologies Pvt. Ltd.
123, Building J2, Shram Seva Premises,
Wadala Truck Terminal, Wadala (E)
Mumbai 400037, Maharashtra, INDIA
E connect@thepencilapp.com
W www.thepencilapp.com

Author biography

First Author Bio:

Kaloian Kirilov

Kaloian (Kal) Kirilov is an entrepreneur with 20 years of experience. He completed his MBA with full scholarship from GVSU, USA, where he worked for the Small Business development center (SBDC) and also for Merrill Lynch. After his return to Bulgaria, he worked for a while in a bank and after that in 2005 set up an own M&A advisory firm, Synergy Group. Mr. Kirilov participated in a lot of M&A deals in his 15 years of consulting experience. He also did management consulting and strategy projects for his clients. The last five years Kal Kirilov developed two own startups so he know what it is to be an entrepreneur from first-hand experience. Mr. Kirilov is also an author of two books about startups which were published in several countries and a book about succession planning.

Second Author Bio:

Professor Sanjay Rout

Professor Doctor Sanjay Kumar Rout is an International Researcher, Innovator, Speaker, Author, Legal Expert, Coach, Editor, Reviewer, Journalist and Policy Expert, Coach. He is well known and highly respected dignitary in the field of Research Development & Innovation working in the major domain of Development Management, Policy Research, Public Policy, Business, Economics, Finance, Law, Social Science, Education, Technology and other Fields. Currently, he is working as Chancellor of MV University (Mexico), Research Director of GIBU University (Liberia), Educational Executive Council member of RKU University, CEO of Innovation Solution Lab, and Director of ISL Publications. He had worked with various national and international organizations in various leadership capacities. Prof. (Dr.) Sanjay Kumar Rout has been a distinguished Researcher, Startup Mentor Innovator, who consistently demonstrates his research work excellence in the field of Research & development, Innovations with greater efficiency, productivity, and quality Innovations & research models., Health, Governance, Technology, Business Management & Academics. He had received many National / International Fellowship & Awards in several categories for his outstanding work in Innovation, Management, Research, Sustainability, and Social Development. He had participated various National/international Summits/Conclave/Seminar/Workshop. He had published 100+ research papers & books.

For his work he had been Honored by many organization as:

Global Influencer in Higher Education Award by CED, GIFT & MSME

Top 50 Global Data & Security Future Thought Leader by Thinkers360

International AOV leadership Award for Research & Innovation Field

World's Best 50 Future Business & Innovation start-up Thought Leader-2020 by Thinkers360

Pillars of India award by ESN Research

Top 50 Global Thought Leaders & Influencers on COVID-19 Business Impact by Thinkers360

Top 50 Global Thought Leaders & Influencers on Public Relation by Thinkers360

Honored as Literary Lieutenant from Story Mirror

Start-up Mentor from Startup World

Best Innovator MUGU International Foundation

Outstanding Global Scientist (Innovation, Author, Policy & Futuristic Speaker) by NCCHWO

Best Author Award from Story Mirror

Best Young Scientist Award from Global Education and Corporate Leadership Awards

Outstanding Researcher Award from Green ThinkerZ

Indira Gandhi Gold Medal Award by GEPRA

Best Guru Award from GECL

Speaker on Public Health at AIDSCON Summit by Postgraduate Institute of Medical Education and Research

Global Speaker on Research Development at WORM-2020 International Summit by Eudoxia Pvt.Ltd

Best Speaker on Artificial Intelligence at Bhartiya Vidyapeeth

His academic credentials contain different achievements from renowned universities/institutions like—NIT, IIM, IIT, University of Pennsylvanian, and University of Washington, Imperial College London, John Hopkins University & others. Including Several achievements, he holds, Three bachelors, Three masters , three Ph.D.& D.Sc. (Medicine) , D.Litt (Law) in his academic career. He is an global certified professional from international acclaimed organization like Google,WHO, BCG,World Bank, Amazon,UNICEF, SAS,UN, European Union, IBM, Asian Development Bank, FAO, Cisco, IRCC,GoI,UNDP & others. And he had worked for various global projects in multiple thematic areas.

AB

CONTENTS

Epigraph

"How to sell your business?" is a book, which reveals all the stages through which an owner has to go through when he decides to find a buyer for his business. The emphasis is on on-going business. Not on selling assets. The book is written based on over 15 years' experience of the author in the field of mergers and acquisitions. As a result the book is not so much a textbook on the subject but it is full of practical cases which every entrepreneur might encounter. The book is written by Mr.Kaloian Kirilov & Professor Sanjay Rout and Publihed by ISL Publications.

You will not find information and advice how the big deals. which the press writes about, are conducted. Instead the described stages and advice are typical for every owner of a family business. This might be a company with 5 mill dollars sales but it can be a company with 200 mill dollars sales. The key is how the business is managed. This will determine the specifics of the M&A process.

"How to sell your business" will help you not only to sell your company but there is also a special section on buying other business. If a family owner decides to take such step it can be costly and that's why it will be wise to be prepared for such important step. The book will not make you an M&A expert but will give you enough foundation so that you can save a lot of money from consultants and also feel comfortable in such talks.

Foreword

Preface

"How to sell your business?" is a book, which reveals all the stages through which an owner has to go through when he decides to find a buyer for his business. The emphasis is on on-going business. Not on selling assets. The book is written based on over 15 years' experience of the author in the field of mergers and acquisitions. As a result the book is not so much a textbook on the subject but it is full of practical cases which every entrepreneur might encounter. The book is written by Mr.Kaloian Kirilov & Professor Sanjay Rout and Publihed by ISL Publications.

You will not find information and advice how the big deals. which the press writes about, are conducted. Instead the described stages and advice are typical for every owner of a family business. This might be a company with 5 mill dollars sales but it can be a company with 200 mill dollars sales. The key is how the business is managed. This will determine the specifics of the M&A process.

"How to sell your business" will help you not only to sell your company but there is also a special section on buying other business. If a family owner decides to take such step it can be costly and that's why it will be wise to be prepared for such important step. The book will not make you an M&A expert but will give you enough foundation so that you can save a lot of money from consultants and also feel comfortable in such talks.

The main topics which are covered in the book are:

1. When and why to sell your business?
2. Steps in the process of selling a company
3. Types of potential buyers
4. How to prepare my company for a sale?
5. What is the value of my business?
6. Structuring the deal
7. Due diligence
8. Integration of a new company
9. How to buy a new business
10. What to do with the money from the sale of the business?

Acknowledgements

We record deep sense of gratitude for my respected all our global Mentor's, Friend and Innovators for all constant direction, helpful discussion and valuable suggestions for writing this book. Due to all valuable suggestions and regular encouragement. We would be able to complete this work and fulfillment of our dream. All our global friends helped us enough during the entire project period like a torch in pitch darkness. We shall remain highly indebted to all throughout our life. We acknowledge our deepest sense of gratitude to our learned parents, who has been throughout a source of Inspiration to us while writing the book. Who helped us at various stages of the writing directly or indirectly. They also enlightened us to follow the path of duty. Special thanks to my children and spouse and almighty for their support in our work.

Introduction

In 2003 I came back from the USA where I completed my MBA with full scholarship. I also worked there two years for the Small Business Development Center and did a MBA internship at Merrill Lynch. When I came back I wanted to work some cool stuff like investment banking but there were not such opportunities in Bulgaria about 20 years ago. After couple years working for some banks in the corporate banking department and at a small Bulgarian boutique financial house I founded my own company for Mergers and Acquisitions – Synergy Group. It was the end of 2005. Time passed by quickly and now I can see that I have worked in the M&A field for 15 years. During all these years I have talked to a lot of Bulgarian entrepreneurs. Most of them don't realize how complex the process of selling a company is or the process of attracting an institutional investor. Very few of them have some knowledge on the subject. This is something normal because we have had private business only the last 30 years. To sell a business is an activity which takes place very seldom in your professional life and very often it is a one-time event. That's why it is understandable that when a person ends up in a similar situation tries to find somebody who has already gone through similar process and to ask him/her for advice. The other option is to improvise and to hope you take the right steps. I have discussed with a lot of owners that the process of selling their business has nothing to do with selling their apartment. In Bulgaria, until that moment there was no summarized information on the topic I decided to write a practical guide, which reveals in details the various steps in the process of selling a company. Since Synergy Group is a Bulgarian M&A boutique most of our deals are related to working with Bulgarian entrepreneurs. We also have worked on some projects for foreign companies but the big deals with multinationals companies which get in the spotlight of the media were not our focus. The main reason is simple. The decisions for any M&A deal is taken at a HQ level so it is hard for a local boutique firm to participate in such deals. As a result, for good or for bad, this allowed us to gain a valuable experience with the deals, which are typical for the small and medium companies. Actually most of the deals we have worked on and closed are considered bigger for Bulgaria. They fall in the range of 3-10 mil euros deals. However the process and the principles are very similar even if you have a smaller business. For example an auto body shop or a restaurant.

There are several reasons why we have chosen to work with bigger companies in Bulgaria. Again this term is a relative because of the size of Bulgaria. Here a company which has sales of 15 mill euros and 2 mill euros EBITDA is considered medium and even big. If you see it through the criteria of the European Union definition than these are small companies.

The main reason why we concentrated on bigger companies is that there is some misunderstanding in most owners about the M&A process itself. Most people believe that a company is sold because it has some financial difficulties or it is close to bankruptcy. At that moment the owner has started to look for options how to save what is left from the business. In such cases we can talk about selling assets but not for selling a business. The terms which the owners can receive in such situation are not satisfactory for them. That wrong perception requires also a big confidentiality when we work on the deals. This is OK and is a normal practice all over the world when we are talking about mergers and acquisitions. It protects all the employees and the clients of the firm. But for the Bulgarian owners it is even much more crucial because. They don't want the outside players to start thinking that he has financial problems because there was an info leak that he is having talks with investors. Sometimes we end up in situations where our team was not presented as a M&A team to the executives and the employees of the firm but as a commercial partner which is negotiating a trading deal.

We are working in the direction to change this wrong perception and one of the goals of the book is to make people more informed about the process of mergers and acquisitions. When it is used and why. At the same time we understand their concerns about confidentiality and that's why in the practical examples I will use I will not mention specific company names. I will make exception only for companies which already don't exist or the information is public.

Whom is this book for?

In order the book to be beneficial to you I will make some clarifications who this book is for and how it can be used. The book is mainly for owners of small and medium businesses and definitely I have in mind private companies. Some of the discussed steps can be used also for public companies but because of the specific regulations of the public companies the process is a little bit different. The book can also be useful for executives at the big multinational companies, which can be part of a similar deal. When an owner decides, for whatever reasons to sell his company, his top executives also are forced to participate actively in the deal. That's why it will be good if they are a familiar with such a process. Last but not least the book can be useful also to all students or people who are interested and want to work in the field of mergers and acquisitions.

Actually when we are talking for mergers and acquisitions the variety of deals is huge and not always we have the classic case when an owner sells 100% of his business. The owner can also sell a stake to a financial investor so that the business can grow much faster. It is possible that the company can have several owners and some of them to change their plans and to want to retire or exit from the business. They can sell their stake to the other shareholders or to new shareholders. The company also can form a new joint venture and of course why not the owner to want to grow not organically and to buy a competitor.

Very often when the press is making some review of the M&A market they include various types of deals. They can include deals with big real estates projects. For example office building, hotels, logistics offices, etc. Although these are also business and have cash flows that types of deals is a little bit different and the buyers are also different. The deal with renewable energy project, solar and wind, are also included in the list of M&A deals. My experience is not so much with that type of deals and that's why my focus will not be much on them.

The book is not written for professional investors and I will not get into technical details and complex financial analysis. On the other side if you are reading the book it will be helpful if you have some basic business knowledge. For example what is an asset, liability or a cash flow and other similar terms. I believe that if you are an owner of a business most probably you are familiar with them and it won't be an issue for you.

The other reason to write the book is at that as a result of Covid-19 issue the world end up in a new financial crisis in 2020. Because of that there will be significant increase of the deals. Unfortunately most of the deals will be for assets not for whole business but even if this is the case it will be good if you are prepared. Of course any deal between private companies can take place any way and without any preparation or strategy. If the two parties are OK with the approach and the terms then we will have an executed deal. Very often the approach when we are talking to owners of small and medium sized companies is that they don't want to initiate an active M&A process. They prefer the play the role of "the unsolicited party". I want to sell my business but will not announce it and will not be the active party. If somebody comes to me and offer me to buy my business I will sit down and will talk to him. If I do this then I will not be perceived as a desperate person and will be able to ask for a higher price. The logic is that in such situation the owner will ask for 10 euros for his business and that's the situation. No room for discussion. There will be no rational explanation or justification why he wants 10 Euro. This is just his desire. At the end the owner says: "I didn't invite the buyer so I don't have to justify it. If he wants my business he has to give me 10 euros or there will be no deal". There is nothing bad with such approach but it is not professional. It looks like that you go to the grocery market to buy cherries and you see an old lady who wants 10 euros for her cherries. If you ask her; "Why do you want 10 euro?" she will tell you: "Because that's how I have decided". However in the M&A you don't sell cherries but a complex business. If you can explain to the buyer that you want 10 euros for your cherries because the fertilizers cost you 3 euros, the water 1 euros, transport 1 euros, and the labor 4 euros you will sound as a person who knows what he is doing. In other words the investors won't perceive you as a craftsman as I like to call the self- made entrepreneurs without putting any negative connotation in the word. You will build a perception in the eyes of the investor that you know what you are doing. This way the potential risks for the buyer will diminish and you will be able to reach better terms for your deal. This book will help you to be better informed but don't expect to give you all answers. Each company is unique and the fact that something happened that way with the deal of your competitor doesn't mean that will be exactly the same with your deal. You know that it is hard to find two identical apartments in a apartment building. What about two complex businesses? The bigger the company the more complex the deal will be. This is also not math because then the deals will be done by computers but whoever is better informed will have an advantage. Haven't you thought why the biggest companies always use consultants when they are buying or selling a business. They have resources, have done many deals, have the preparation and despite everything when Coca-Cola is making a deal it always uses consultants or investment bankers. At the same time John who has a small production for juices doesn't use it. He wants 10 euros for his business and if somebody gives them to him there will be a deal. If nobody offers him the asked price he hopes that Coca Cola won't force him to go out of business because they have economy of scale and all necessary resources. If that happen then he will have to sell assets at a later stage because not much business will be left. It is a little bit strange such behavior, isn't it? However that is the reality and not only in Eastern Europe where I come from.

Yes, I, as a M&A advisor I am subjective in making such statement but from my 15 years of practice in the field I see that it is much easier to work with people who are informed in the process. They know what it is the benefit to follow some advice. What will be the consequences of some of their actions, etc. I hope this book also helps them in that process and to get an expertise in the field. The entrepreneurs should understand that the M&A consultants are not brokers and their added value is not the fact that they can find John who will buy your business. Actually unlike the brokers, the M&A consultants have to sit down on one side of the table and to help and advice only one party in the process. Unlike the real estate brokers who expect to get commission from both sides because they matched the buyer and the seller. For the role of the M&A consultants will talk in more details later in the book.

How is the book organized?

The whole book is organized as a practical guide with 12 chapters which cover all steps in the process of selling or buying a company. We start with the question when and why to sell? The preparation of such process, then we go and discuss who might be the various types of potential buyers of your business, how to structure and negotiate your deal, talk about the complex word "due diligence" which everybody is talking about and we end up with the closing of the deal. It is not less important also what happens with the company after the deal is signed because this is the moment when most deals in the M&A process turn into unsuccessful projects. It is also important to discuss what you can do when you cash out and you end up with no business and one bag full of money in your hand. I also included a whole chapter for the people who wants to grow not organically and are ready to buy another business. Either to expand their current business or just to diversify it with other sectors. Some of the steps are identical with the ones in the selling process but there are some specifics. Some entrepreneurs are intimidate to buy another business but very often this might be the better strategy compared to starting a business from scratch. This applies even to a bigger extend if you want to step on foreign markets. A lot of owners in Eastern Europe are intimidated to buy businesses in Western Europe or in the USA but the reality is that in the developed markets they can even sign better deals than in Eastern Europe.

At the moment there are not many practical guides out there on the market and I will try, as much the confidentiality clauses allow me, to prepare you for such a process if you are the owner of a small or medium business.

Chapter 2
When and Why to sell?

When and Why to Sell

When to sell?

Any consultant can help you in the process of selling or buying a company. That's his expertise and he knows the steps in details. There is something for which nobody can help you and you have to take the decision by yourself. This is the decision when to sell your business. Based on my 15 years experience in the field I can tell you that when an owner is not internally convinced that this is the right step almost never the process ends up successfully. When is the best time to sell? There is no exact answer. Nobody can tell you with 100% certainty. Even entrepreneurs who have completed successful exits sometimes believe that they could have done better. In general the best time to sell your company is when it is on top or actually when it is climbing to the top and all the forecasts for its development are very bright. At that moment you can generate the biggest interest from potential buyers and to receive the best possible price. The paradox is that exactly at the moment the owners feel very strong. They don't think about selling and actually it doesn't make sense to them to sell at that particular moment. It requires a great internal discipline and sometimes the help of some outside factors for which we will talk in a little bit, in order to decide to sell your business in such situation. I remember that when we worked on the deal with Devorex the company was developing very well. It had a huge increase in sales and in profits during the last 2-3 years. The owner had just built a new factory and moved the production there. One of the potential buyers even was surprised why they are selling now when they just moved in and have not yet used the potential of the new factory and the investments they have made. We had an identical situation when the owners of the confectionery producer Prestige - 96 sold their company. They had a great financial results and they just built a new factory which they were going to move in very soon after the deal. In the first case we had owners which we can define them as serial entrepreneurs. Those are people which create a business, develop it to some stage and they sell it successfully to somebody else. In the second case we had owners which had only one business which was like a kid to them but they had received an offer to which they couldn't resist. In both cases the deals took place when the companies were getting to the top of their development. If there is something which you can say for sure is that a good time is when you have the time of your life in terms of financial results of the firm. In Bulgaria in most cases when the business is doing well the owners feel confident and they tell you that if they have a good offer they would sell but actually in practice they never do it. Their expectations for price are so high at that moment that they look outrages to the buyers. This is normal human reaction in such situation. Owners expect that somebody like Santa Clause will come with the big bag with money and will give it to them. This happens from time to time like was the case of Prestige-96 but it is not the normal practice. At the end nobody says that Mercedes is a bad car but does it worth the price or it is better to have two Toyatas for the price of one Mercedes. However, when the business for objective or subjective reasons start experiencing difficulties then the owners start looking for potential buyers. Usually in such situation the business has gone to a downward spiral from which it is hard to get out. Because their business is declining the potential buyers are worried and that's why they offer discounted valuations. The owners are not pleased with such valuation and they decide to wait a little bit more hoping that things can get better or that some idiot investor will come and give them a better price. If the entrepreneurs don't take actions to stabilize the company and do some restructuring, which is not always easy because of objective reasons, their sales and profits continue to go down. The investors start feeling even more worried and they decrease their offers even further. Very often as a result the owners are forced to sell assets or if they have a lot of bank loans then the bank takes control over the company and the bank itself starts selling off all assets in order to get back part of the loans they had given. Perhaps, cases like this which are very often, created this perception in Bulgaria that if a business is for sale this means that it has financial difficulties or there is something which is not right. There is something which is hidden and which will show up at a later stage once the investor has bought the company. Otherwise why an entrepreneur will sell a very profitable company? There are several objective reasons for that step and we will discuss them in a little bit but the main reason is to reduce the risk. The wise men say: "It will not always be like that". As the bad periods at some point ends also the good periods don't continue forever. Now an interesting example comes to my head. This is the procedure for the concession of Sofia Airport where we were helping the one of the interesting investors. It is true that when we are talking for privatization deals there are also non-economic factors but the Bulgarian government long time was waiting and didn't start the procedure. The Belgrade airport which is smaller than Sofia airport was given under concession in 2017 and the Serbian government did a very good deal in terms of a strategic investor and the money it received. In 2018 the government started the process for a second time but it got delayd and in the middle of 2020 the deal is not closed yet. Now because of the Covid-19 situation which will have very long term effects on the avio industry I don't know how the investors will react. Actually we have a chosen buyer but the deal was not closed officially since some of other investors contest the decision in the court. Perhaps the government got lucky in the last moment since they got a binding offer but my point was that if they delayed it several more months and with this Covid situation there will be years till the market normalize in the sector. A man never knows how the situation will change in the future. If at the moment an owner believes that he can double his business within 3-4 years with the same probability the business can also disappear completely for the same period of time. About 10 years ago we worked on a deal about fright rail manufacturer. The company was doing very well and was profitable. At the time there was a huge shortage of freight rail wagons and the Bulgarian state railway company was wondering what to do and how to serve the demand of the manufacturers for wagons. Back then the owners of our client decided that besides refurbishing of wagons they can also start manufacturing brand new freight wagons. They had found a big international company which signed a contract with them for the manufacturing of 800 brand new wagons. The contract was with fixed prices, guaranteed work and cash flows for the next several years. The company had to build a new production hall which would take about a year before the first wagons were produced but that time was included in the contract so everything was planned very well. The owners had already started building the new production hall but at the same time they wanted to attract also a foreign investor in the company. We organized the process and we had over 10 visits from various investors. Some of them were strategic investors and others were investment funds. There was a huge interest. Very seldom we had managed to generate such an interest towards a Bulgarian company. However let's not forget that everything was just yet only on papers. The signed contract, the plans and the production hall had to be built. The investors considered some risks and normally discounted their offers for those risks. Some of the offers were not so bad but they didn't meet the expectations of the owners. The idea was that once we built the new factory and produce the first new freight wagons then many of those risk would disappear and the investors will increase their offers for the acquisition. That was good as a plan but then the financial crisis of 2008 came. The business of almost all companies shrank and the business didn't need so many wagons. All of a sudden from a huge shortage of freight wagons the transportation companies had spare wagons. Since the Bulgarian company had some delays with building the new production hall and the first wagons, the foreign company used that delay and decreased the number of the wagons which they were going to buy. I am saying it was with multiple of times not percentage. It was a huge change in the contract. That's normal but the whole investment project and the loans which were taken from the banks were forecasted for the volume of production which was in the initial contract. That's how the company started in the downward spiral for which I was talking about. There were also other factors but at the end this company got into very difficult financial situation and in several years it bankrupt and disappear. That's why the main reason a person to sell when he has a very profitable business is that he has no warranty that it will be like this in two or three years.

A person can get into the other extreme situation when we have a financial crisis like we did in 2008-2009. It looks like that we will have it also now because of the Covid-19 situation. Because there is a lot of uncertainty and fear in the investor the prices of all assets and business is going down during such financial crisis. It doesn't matter what type of business you have. It will be very hard to receive the valuation which you could receive in 2018 for example. A pure psychological reaction. Clients with which I am working with for a long time tell me that it is not the moment to sell right now. I am telling them that they might be right in general but it all depends on what they want to do. Yes, for sure if they could sell their business for 1000 euros two years ago there will be no way to receive the same valuation in 2020 or 2021. If they have a good business perhaps they can get 800 euros. However in absolute numbers they would be a paper loss. At the same time because of the crisis some businesses will have bigger problems and their valuation will go down much more significantly. So if you sell your business now and you keep the money in the bank you will loose from that deal and better not sell it during the crisis. But if you use the crisis then with these 800 euros you will be able to buy assets or companies for which you could only dream about 2 years ago. They would cost a lot more than 1000 euros which was the valuation of your business in 2018. It is normal. The prices of the good companies and assets go down with smaller percentage during a crisis than the valuation of the more troubled or leveraged businesses.

When and why to sell also depends to a huge extend and to the fact if you have several businesses or this is your only company which you have started from scratch and it is like your child. If you are reading this book most probably you have some type of business and you know very well that your business is really like a child. In such situation it is very hard to take a decision to sell it. When you have several companies, it doesn't matter if you love them very much the feeling for them is more of a business and it is much easier to sell one of them.

When to sell also depends if you will organize something like formal process with auction or you will have private unsolicited talks with a potential buyer. When you have an auction you have a carefully thought through decision and a preparation for the process. In other words you are prepared and you control if and when to sell. In most cases with the so call craftsmen from me they have commercial partners who at some point of time offers them to buy their business. Then the whole process is a little bit ad hoc.

Reasons why to sell your company

Now I will discuss over 10 reasons why an owner is ready to sell his business but I am sure you can come up with even more items. Very often the decision is a combination of several reasons. Go through these cases and think if they apply for you. If that is the case then you can seriously think about the idea to sell your company.

 You are tired. Under this denominator can go many of the cases at least we at Synergy Group have worked on. A significant part of the Bulgarian private companies are founded in the 90s, after the communism. They were either privatized from the state owned enterprises or were Greenfield investments. After the owners have done business for over 20 years now they are very exhausted. Not so much physically but psychologically. You know how big responsibility is to create a business and to take care of employees and clients. Have also in mind that many of the owners couldn't build a corporate structures in their companies. This didn't allow them to hire professional managers which to take over the operating activities. As a result the owners were under everyday pressure for 20 years and this is not easy to handle. They usually tell me that they are ready to stay in the company on a more strategic role and to help but they don't want to "drive the train" anymore.

 Necessity of significant investments in the business. Perhaps your business has reached a stage where a significant investments has to be made. It might be for new machines, new production hall, or for starting a new line of business. If you don't do it you know that your business will not be so competitive anymore. Your revenues and profits will decrease, your business will shrink and can even disappear in several years. Perhaps if you don't want to take this risk with the new big investment to let somebody else to take over and he will continue the fight with your competitors.

A big company has just acquired one of your competitors. Let's take the following example. Let's imagine that in a district city there are two local retail food chains. One of them is yours. For many years you compete with you neighbor. Sometimes it is more successful and sometimes you have more difficulties but you manage to develop and grow the business during all these years. One day a big multinational retail chain with deep pockets is buying your local competitor. Now the game will be more similar to the fight between David and Goliath. You can try to keep fighting alone but if you want to maximize the value of your business it might be better to think about selling it or to attract a big financial partner who will join your company as a shareholder.

The heirs are not interested in the business. Most companies in Bulgaria and all over the world are family businesses. When you have worked 15-20 years on a project and it is successful the biggest joy for any parent is to leave the company to his heirs so that they can continue his work. Sometimes this works out well. There are numerous cases in the world for family companies which managed to transfer the ownership from one generation to another generation. In Eastern Europe now is the moment when we witness the first wave of transferring the ownership and management between the family generations. Many of the kids of the local entrepreneurs are already grown up people and they are ready to take over the wheel. Here two problems can arise and they are typical not only for the companies in Eastern Europe. The only difference is that we in Bulgaria witness this process for the first time while in Western Europe it is not something new and people have some experience how to handle it. The first problem is that the kids might not be interested to work and develop the business of their parents. It is normal. Every person has different interests. The fact that the parents have set up a tour operator doesn't mean that their kids wants to develop the business at all. Perhaps the kid might want to become a musician or to develop a different kind of business. For example something related to technology and to set up their own startup. One of the options which the entrepreneurs have is to force their kids to take over the business but very often the results won't be very good. The reason is that kid won't work with the same passion as you do because he/she doesn't love what you are doing. Under the term "Force" I don't mean a direct order for your kids to take over the business from you. For example you have several times mentioned in the family that you are developing the business for them. You have sent them abroad to study business and they know that one day when they come back they are "supposed" to take over the business. If you raised your kids well and they are responsible people they will not reject this expectation. The question is if they will be happy to continue your efforts. Perhaps it is better to sell the business and with part of the proceeds your kids can go and try make their dreams come true. Whatever they are. The other potential problem with the heirs is if they have the skills and capabilities to take over the business from you and run it successfully.

The fact that you have sent them to the best business schools doesn't automatically means that they will be as successful as you are. To become a manager you can learn that skill in the business school. To be an entrepreneur, at least in more opinion, it is more of a set of born skills. You can develop them but in most cases either you have it until you finish high school or you don't. If you haven't learned to set goals by yourself and to chase them until you reach them or to wake up early in the morning by yourself not because your dad wakes you up 5 times not to be late for school it cannot be learned at later stage. These things depends more of the character of the person and of course of the upbringing but once the period for learning pass it is hard to fix it. A married woman tries to change his husband for 20 years but know that it is impossible. In such situation the responsibility for that decision falls entirely on the parents. This is the hardest choice they have to make. I don't want to give specific examples but there some Bulgarian big companies which were ruined because of the incompetent management once the heirs took over the company. I am sure that each of you in your country can find also such examples. However, since this process is not new in Western Europe and they have seen the possible bad consequences of handling their business to hers which don't have the skills. As a result the owners hire some professional managers who take over the operating work and the entrepreneurs are becoming just shareholders in the companies. In Eastern Europe since we are now doing this cycle for the first time we have to see though personal experience that this is viable case (our kids are not capable to run our business successfully) so that the owners think about the option of professional managers as a complete viable option.

The company doesn't grow significantly anymore – If your business has reached to a certain stage and doesn't grow anymore perhaps you don't possess the necessary skills or capital to take it to the next level of development. As we discussed it is one thing to start a business or run a small company and completely different thing to run a big corporation.

In the big corporations the business happens in a different way and it requires a different set of skills. You are an entrepreneur but perhaps your business needs now more a manager. If you don't possess the skills of a manager perhaps it is better to sell your business now instead of taking a chance to start losing clients and revenues. This might be the more probable outcome than the business to stay stable during the next 4-5 years.

You have health problems – Sometimes it just happens that a person has health problems. I mean more long-term problem not catching a flu. At the same time your kids are still young and you cannot leave the business to them. You also don't have a prepared professional manager who can run the business instead of you with the same success. You are left with no other option besides to sell your business. The sell itself will take several month and even a year so this step is not the right one if your health problems can be solved within a year. But if your health problems are more long-term than the only option is find another owner of the business and to take care of yourself.

There are businesses which depends too much on one client or an employee. If this is the case and you lose that client or employee perhaps it is the better option to find another owner who can take over and try to turnaround the business before it is too late and it goes to bankruptcy.

The M&A market is very hot. You know that economy develops in cycles. There are always years when everything develops very well, the perspective is optimistic, people don't think so much about the risks and believe that it will be like that forever. The past period of 2013-2019 is a great example. Also the 2001-2008 period. As I wrote in the previous chapter when you are at the top and everything is bed of roses not only you become so optimistic but also the investors do. Another supporting factor is when the central banks are trying to solve some issues and are printing money like crazy. This behavior continues already a decade. We end up with a huge amount of free cash which has to go somewhere. All these factors lead to increase of the valuations of the companies. If you are in such market perhaps it will be better to make use of the situation and to sell so that you can cash at the maximum valuation. If you still want to deal with some business you can buy later on another business when the down cycle comes and the valuations are much lower. Many people have turn this strategy in their business. Even in the real estate business is like that. You sell at the top when everybody is buying because the prices are going up and they are buying when everybody is scared and doesn't see any light at the end of the tunnel.

A very strong competitor has recently adopted a strategy to expand its market share. The big corporations which also have very deep pockets sometimes intentionally sell their products even under cost so that they can take a market share and kick out some of their smaller competitors out of the market. If they managed to do it then later on the companies will be able to raise their prices in a situation with much smaller competition. You can see this strategy to be applicable not only when we are talking for companies but also with countries. Let's look the situation with the petrol. countries like Russia, Saudi Arabia and others which from time to time try keep the petrol prices so low that they hope some of their competitors will go bankrupt. In general this strategy is against the law (to sell under your COGS) but it is hard to prove. If you witness such practice in your sector and in your market you have to ask yourself how deep pockets you have and how long you can participate in such price war. Perhaps it will be wiser to sell at that moment. Actually if you see such strategy in place I would call that big competitor and would tell him: "I know what you are doing. Perhaps it is better the money which you will spend in order to take me out of business to give it to me by buying my business. This way it will be better for both companies.

Complete a cycle. There are people who are serial entrepreneurs. They start a business from scratch or buy an existing business, develop it to a certain point, and then they sell it. It is like a business itself for them. Such people are the former owners of Devorex which before that company had two other businesses in completely different industries. After they sold Devorex the owners had plans to start a fourth business in a new industry. For that type of entrepreneurs it is a normal thing to sell the business, to close the cycle, and to start a new one.

Several owners. A lot of companies have more than one shareholder. They are not family businesses. This is normal in the business world where to have founders who have different skill set or resources. This way the business is more prepared to handle the competition. However things change over time. The different people have different interest and goals. If one of the founders wants to take over the world but the other founder is tired and wants to cash out then this a reason for heated arguments between them how to run the business. Sometimes people change and this also leads to difference in how the business to be run. It is like in the marriage. There is no way to know how things will develop in 5-10 years. If you know that you will divorce in 10 years you wouldn't marry the first time but nobody knows. I have been a witness how 5-6 owners are working together for 20 years with no serious problems and at the same time how two brothers got into fight and have to divide the business. Everything is very individualistic. If you end up in such situation and your relationship is compromised or you just have different ambitions and goals then one of the working solution is one of the owners to sell his stake and to get out of the business. He can sell it to a new shareholder or the more probable option is to sell his stake to the other shareholders in the business. Very often the shareholders agreements have such clauses which force one of the founders to offer their stake first to the other founders so this is a normal practice in the business world. Besides if you a new person to the company and you are not a professional investor as the investment funds it will be a high risk step to enter a new company with founders and business you don't know. But this is more the perspective and the issues for the new investor. From time to time we at Synergy Group have deals where one of the founders sell his stake to the other founders.

Take over the world. Sometimes your company is developing well but not as fast as your ambitions. In other words you want to take over the world. In such situations very often the owners are selling a stake in the company to an investment fund (It can be a private equity fund or a venture capital fund depending on the stage of the business) so that the business can grow much faster. With their help you can achieve your goals within 2-3 years instead of 5-6 if you trying to do it just by yourself. That was the case with Jet Credit which is a consumer finance company and one of the most successful deals in Bulgaria about 10 years ago. Nowadays we also have similar deals where successful companies sell a minority and more seldom a majority stake to an investment fund so that they can grow faster and have resources to compete on the world market.

JV (joint venture). In most examples in the book we are talking for selling or buying a business but the first word in the abbreviator of M&A is about mergers. The mergers or the joint ventures as number of deals are lot smaller than the acquisitions but they still exist. It is normal practice when you are trying to enter a foreign market to sign some type of joint venture with a local player. The key here is from the very beginning to set up clear terms how you could "divorce" if you get disagreement or the JV has achieved its goals and is not needed anymore.

Divorce. We said that nowadays about 50% of the marriages end up with a divorce. Very often the family companies are joint companies. I mean that even formally your wife can have some stake in the company. Just to show her that you are doing this together. Even if you didn't gave your spouse a formal stake still according to most legislations everything which is acquired or developed as assets during the marriage is considered joint ownership. With the companies it is a little bit different because they are a separate legal entities but still they might have rights from the proceeds of the business if you sell it. This a legal issue and I am not a lawyer. Besides it might differs according the legislation in the different countries. However, you got my point. If you have some personal problems and your spouse is a formal shareholder in the company then you might be force to sell the whole company. With divorce there are a lot of emotions and people don't think rationally. If they cannot divide the business very often the spouses take the decision to sell the company because it is easier to divide the money.

There are cases when your business is local and you are forced to move for a long time to a different location for whatever reasons. It might be health reasons or just want to go to live in a warmer country. Sometimes people from Eastern Europe or Russia are fed up with the corruption and the bureaucracy in their countries and they decide to move to the USA or Western Europe. Then you have a problem. What to do with the business? You can try to keep developing and controlling it from a distance but the smaller the business is the harder it will be. That's why a normal outcome in such situation is to sell your local business (for example a restaurant) and with the proceeds from the sell to open a new restaurant in the new location.

Need of money for a new business. Sometimes you see a new opportunity on the market and want to start a new business. You believe that the perspective for this new business is much bigger than that of your current business but don't have the capital to start. Then you sell your current business and with the money you start your new business.

Inheritance. Sometimes life is not fair and because of a car accident or another accident the owner or the people who run the business die. In such situation you can become the owner of a new big company which you don't know what to do with. If there is no written will and there are several heirs the things can become even more complex. First you might not have the skills to develop the business or might have no interest. So far you haven't done anything about the company and most probably it is like that because you are not interested in its activities. A couple similar cases in Bulgaria come to my head right now. In such cases when you inherit a business because of the lack of skills, interest and most probably a conflict with the other heirs to sell the business while it is still working is the wisest decision.

Change in the lifestyle. Sometimes, although not very often, I have witnessed cases when a person changes completely his lifestyle. This can make it difficult the operation of your business. For example more often this happens with women who got married, have kids and now their priorities in their lives are others.

Divestures. This situation as a case is more common for the big companies not so much for the entrepreneurs who have their own business and who are the main target of the book. Imagine a situation where a corporation with several businesses decided to get rid of some of the line of businesses because it is not its core business. For example by default the mangers always want to manage bigger companies because they feel more important. The economic situation is favorable, they decide to expand into other niches and buy different businesses. Sometimes things don't work out well. The reason can be objective (the business environment gets worse) or it can be subjective. Most probably not good integration of the new business and we will have a whole chapter about this issue later in the book. Even if the worse business environment is the reason the board takes a decision the company to get rid off the non-strategic division of the company. First you have bought this division and now you are trying to sell it. This game never ends and is repeated usually with every economic cycle. In the smaller countries where the companies are not so big and don't have several business divisions these divestures are not so often but in Western Europe and the USA it is common and even most deals are divesture type.

As you can see the list with reasons to sell a company is not small and can be even added with additional items. However it is important to note that in order to be able to react to these reasons an owner has to be prepared for a process of mergers and acquisitions. There is no way how things can work out well if you rely only on luck. Most small and medium business are not prepared and that's why we have a separate chapter on the topic.

When you decide if and when to sell your company you have to take into consideration two other key components. Which one is more important for you? The money or time. Some of the reasons above require the sale to happen fast and then the time for which you will find a buyer for your business is very crucial. In other cases I have seen that the amount of money is the key factor. With Synergy Group we had several cases where the owners are so tired already and want to sell their business badly but at the same time are fixed on a predetermined price which cause the deal to fall apart. If you think it carefully you have an owner who has created a business. Worked for 15-20 years and now is very tired. He wants to take a rest and if he sell the business either for 7 or for 10 mill euros it wouldn't matter so much for his financial status. In both cases neither he nor his kids will be starving. I think the reason why the owners are so fixed on the valuation of their company is not so much the money but they accept it as some type a benchmark for their success. For their efforts and what they have achieved for that period of time. It is one thing to have created a business which was sold for 7 mill euros and another perception if you sell it for 10 mill euros. In the second case your friends will say: Wow, Kaloian did such a great deal. He managed to sell his company for 10 mill euros. Great business and great deal". If you sell it for 7 mill euros then somebody might say: "well nothing special, look at John he had same business and sold it for 10 mill euros". It is normal human desire to receive a recognition for your efforts. The question is if this has to be a break dealer. Obviously the owner doesn't feel the pleasure to wake up every morning and keep developing his business. But he also wants to receive the deserved recognition which come with the valuation. Where is the balance? Nobody can tell for sure. Every entrepreneur will decide for himself when he puts the time on one side of the scale and the money on the side of the scale.

The other important moment is if you care who will buy your business. There are entrepreneurs who don't care who will buy their companies and what will happen with them after the deal. I don't mean that you have to sell your business to people who are considered criminals but not to be so picky about the buyer. For example you can sell the company to a big multinational firm which you know that they don't need your production facilities. It is very likely that once they buy your firm to shut down the factory and a lot of people will be out of job. Many of these people you had known for years and you won't be very happy if you disappoint them. That's why you have to decide if this issue is of importance to you when choosing the buyer. If it is not of significance then you will choose the highest valuation especially if we are talking for 100% sale. If it matters then the situation become more complex and you have to be very careful and to structure the deal in a way which will guarantee that something like this won't happen.

Steps in the Sell Process of a Company

A man doesn't wake up one morning with the thought: "I will start the process of selling my company tomorrow". There is a preparation phase and that's why it is difficult to say exactly how much time the whole process takes. The time and the steps depends on the fact if you will make an auction or just one of your commercial partners all of a sudden will make you a proposal to buy your business. In the second situation many of the steps and also the time can be shortened. Besides the different stages also depends whether you will sell the whole company or just a part of it. In the previous chapter we discussed over ten reasons which can lead to taking such decision and each of them has its specifics. That's why a person cannot come up with a universal approach which can be used in all cases. Now I will discuss in more details the case when a company owner decides to organize an intentional sale process for his company and also wants to organize an auction. In other words to invite as many as possible potential buyers which will make offers. Here how such process goes through:

Step 1 Preparation of the company

A process of mergers and acquisitions will run more smoothly and will have bigger chance to be successful if the company is prepared for it. Some of the businesses are run in such way that they need little or no preparation. Other business however will need a lot of preparation before they can launch the process. You can start the process with making you financials clean and official, go through the step of taking some of your personal assets out of the company as a legal entity, and end up with the pure technical steps which are necessary. Here you can include also the choice of a team, which will lead the process. What part of the team will be comprised of people form the company and what part will be outside consultants, which has to be hired is also part of preparation. You have to prepare a teaser of the company and an information memorandum. Without such documents you cannot lead a serious process of M&A. it will be also a very good step to have a prepared valuation of the company by a M&A consultant. The whole preparation is very important and it can take a significant time. That's why we will have a separate chapter just on this step.

Step 2. Preparing a list of potential buyers for your business

After you have prepared your company and have all necessary documents you have to make an initial list with all potential buyers for your business. In general the bugger part of the work on the M&A process should be done by your M&A consultant. You as an owner can take over all the tasks of the process but have in mind that it takes a lot of time. Meanwhile somebody has to manage the company and to do the operating work. Even if you hire consultants they cannot do the whole work just by themselves. First because they don't have an executive power and secondly they don't know the business as well as you do. That's why you have to work together. Even for steps for which it is assumed that they should be done entirely by the consultant. At the end both parties have a common interest. To find a buyer who will give a maximum price for the company. The list of potential buyers will include financial buyers such as private equity funds and also strategic players. Here it does matter if you sell the whole business or just part of it with the idea to grow faster. In regards to the strategic buyers you have to sit down together with your consultant and jointly to prepare a list of all companies in your sector which would have the financial resources to buy your business. If the deal is supposed to be around 5 mill euros there is no point to include companies which cannot afford to pay such amount. Unless the potential buyer is part of a bigger holding or his owner also has other business. Sometimes the buyer can be a company which at first sight doesn't look like to have synergy with your business but you never know what is in the head of its owners or executives. Perhaps they might have decided to enter a new niche. It will be wise to prepare a list of at least 50-60 companies and to divide the list into two parts. Potential buyers with priority (or list A) and in the B group you will put companies which doesn't look so likely to buy your business. You can start with the first group but if the interest is not so big as you have expected then gradually you can also contact companies from the second list. This list is not a closed one. During the process you can come up with other ideas or remember companies which you have forgotten to include it the first place so you can say that it will be open list, work in progress.

Step 3. Contact with the potential buyers

Once you have the initial list of the companies it has to be filled with the contact details of the companies and the decision makers of those companies. Who are the people who takes the decisions? Their personal e-mails and phones if it is possible. What investment does the potential buyer has in similar companies? What are its financial results? The more information you have for the potential buyer the better for you. You cannot rely just on your consultant to fill this data. Better help him also with information. If you have chosen company A as a potential buyer there is no point for him to contact them by sending e-mail to office@companyABC.com It will better if you give him the e-mail or the phone of the owner or some of the key executives there. This way you not only will save time but you will control the whole process much better because the secretary in the office of the potential buyer will not find out about the deal. Of course the good consultants already have established contacts with the financial investors and with some of the strategic players especially if they already have worked on a deal in the same sector. Here you can have two approaches. In the active one you call the executives of the potential buyers and in the passive one you send them an e-mail. There is no problem to use both approaches simultaneously depending on your relationship with the potential investor.

Step 4 Send the teaser

The teaser is a short document of 1-2 pages which describes the main parameters of your company and the potential deal. Whether the whole company is offered for acquisition or just a stake from it. Is the deal is for cash out or the capital will be increased with the new investment, etc? This short document is anonymous and doesn't reveal the name of the presented company. If you are in small country like Bulgaria sometimes it might be hard to hide the identity of the company, especially if we are talking for some of the bigger local firms. For example how many pharmaceutical companies or TV channels you will have? Nothing cannot be done in this situation and you have to accept the fact that some people can figure out the identity of the company even with just the blind teaser in hand.

Step 5. Signing of the confidentiality agreement

If the potential buyers which you have contacted express interest in your investment opportunity they would like to receive more detail information about it. That type information is usually in the information memorandum of the company. The confidentiality agreement has a goal to guarantee you that the potential investors will not share it with other unauthorized people once they receive it. The idea is the news for potential sell not to hurt your business. There are various types of confidentiality agreements. Some of them are harsher with financial penalties and others are easier on the signing parties. This document you can also see it under the name NDA (non-disclosure agreement). In the appendix you can see a draft of an example of a confidentiality agreement. Here I will disagree a little bit with the lawyers about the confidentiality agreements and I think that their role is a little bit exaggerated. At least in the Eastern European countries. First, whatever draft the potential investor signs it is very hard to sue him in the court in case of information leak. In order to succeed in court you must have written proofs like e-mails or some documents. The practice shows that in most cases the leak of information takes place orally. Pretty much two people have a meeting in the coffee shop and one of them mentions that company A is looking for an investor. Usually people from the same sector sits down and they discuss the gossips between themselves. Everybody is doing it. It is very hard to prove it.

The second element is that even if you prove that the information leak was from Mr. X you also have to prove that you have suffered some financial loss from the fact that the society found out that you are looking for an investor for your business. If you cannot prove financial losses then the court will not put financial fine on that person who revealed an information unless the amount of the penalty is specified in the agreement explicitly. Then you just have to prove the act of breach. Here we are talking for a private information not an info which got out in the media. I assume in each country there are speculations that some of the companies are looking for investors. It is something like public secret. What will be the financial loss for the company if you mentioned something about the deal? It is already public news. That's why for me the NDA actually acts more the role of a gentlemen agreement and it will have reputation consequences on the potential investor if the word goes out that he is acting like this. Next time nobody will want to do M&A deal with him or at least will be very careful. With my interpretation of the NDA I don't want to say that I underestimate the importance of this document but it depends a lot on the actions and the experience of the M&A consultant. If he puts an ad for the sale of your company on some platforms for M&A deals it is normal that the word will go out much faster. However, it depends again on the type of company which is for sale. If you will sell the biggest telecom in the country then the negotiations are in private talks but if you have to sell a small restaurant it is normal to announce it on some specialized platforms. What I am telling our clients is that most likely the info about the deal will not be out in the media but most probably some people in their sector will find out because people are talking between themselves. Sometimes not intentionally. It is just gossips for them.

Step 6. Sending the information memorandum

After the confidentiality agreement is signed you send the information memorandum to the interested investor. The memorandum is a detail presentation of your company which should answer most questions which a potential investor would have. If the document is 20 slides PowerPoint presentation or 50 pages word documents depends on how big and complex is business, which will be sold and also from other factors. It is possible that you didn't manage to cover all topics in the IM and the potential buyer can send you additional questions about your company. The idea is based on the IM the investor to receive a roughly idea about the value of your business.

Sometimes in the more structured processes the seller might request from the interested buyers to submit an indicative, non-binding offer, for the company just based on the information they have received from the Information memorandum. The idea is to screen out the more serious investors because when you organize an auction it is not easy to negotiate with a dozen potential buyers. With the deals we have done in Bulgaria this happens rarely because the deals are smaller and they cannot generate so big interest from foreign buyers. Besides it is not normal for me to buy a business just based on some papers. It is like to buy an apartment just based on pictures of it. Besides you sell a company which is very dependable on its founders. We are talking mainly for family owned businesses. To buy such company without meeting the owner and see how he thinks and manage the business is not serious. For the big international companies it might be a different story. Because of these reasons after the IM is sent usually the process goes to its next step.

Step 7. Meeting with the potential buyers and negotiations.

After the potential buyer had received the Information memorandum usually he requests to go and visit the company especially if there are some assets. It is a production company, not a services company like IT. This step takes the longest time. It can take several months. You as an owner can try to accelerate the process by putting a deadline for the next stage which is submitting binding offers. This depends in how strong position you are. How big is the interest and how many potential investors are in the process? If you put a deadline you take a chance that a potential investor who might give you a good offer to be left out of the process because he didn't meet the deadline. At this stage you provide additional information to the investors, negotiate the terms and the price of the company. It is also a good moment to present the valuation of the company which your consultants had prepared in advance. Of course the buyer will decide by himself if he will agree with the valuation but at least it can serve as a starting point for the negotiations. You also structure the deal at this stage and the price is not the only term which you have to agree on. Even if you are selling 100% of your business still there are other important issues which have to be negotiated. All these steps has to be done simultaneously with all interested buyers. The tricky part is that it is very difficult to be at the same stage of the negotiations with all interested buyers. Even if you start at the same time with all buyers each company has a different style of taking decisions and different pace. Here comes the role and the added value of the M&A consultant who has to manage the process very well.

Step 8 receiving the offers

After you have talked several weeks, and more often several months with the potential buyers comes the moment to put an end of this stage and to set up a deadline for receiving binding offers. The practice here is the offers to be binding. However since the due diligence process still didn't take place most investors put clauses in their binding offers that they are subject to due diligence. In other words they put such clauses which allows them to change their offer in such way that it might become unacceptable to you. Let's stay positive and let's hope that you will have several binding offers on the table. Now you as an owner has to choose the buyer with whom you would like to continue down in the process. Depending on your goals you can weighed the price and the other terms of the offers and choose the best one for you. I have been a witness that sometimes the owner doesn't pick the offer with the highest price. This happens mostly when he is not selling 100% of the company but just part of it. After you choose the potential investor the normal practice is to give him exclusivity for some period of time. This period in most cases is 2-3 months and you have to let the other investors know that you have chosen a preferred buyer. It is important to let them know that although you had chosen somebody else if things don't work out with him and you don't close the deal you will come back and can continue the process with them. Just to keep your door open.

Step 9. Due Diligence

This famous phrase which is usually very hard to be translated on your local language means that the chosen investor will check if the information you have given to him actually is correct. Let's not forget that he based his offer entirely on the information and the facts you have presented to him and they might not be really true or at least to be bended a little bit in your favor. So at this stage with the help of auditors and lawyers, the chosen buyer will have access to your documentation so that he can check the truth of the received information. In the bigger transaction the companies usually use virtual data room but there is no problem the buyer to come to your office and to do the diligence in person. After the buyer conducts the due diligence process we might have two options. The discrepancies which the buyer found in the information are not significant and he didn't find any skeletons in the wardrobe as is the jargon in the M&A world. In that case he will be ready confirm his offer or to negotiate some small changes with you and you can move to the next stage, signing the contract. However, if he got scared by something which he had found in the due diligence and wants to change significantly his initial offer then you have to come back one step back and check if any of the other investors who had submitted binding offers is still interested to close the deal with you. If there is such investor then you give him exclusivity so that he can do due diligence. Again you close the negations window with the other interested buyers.

Step 10. Preparing of the share purchase agreement

Here is the stage where the lawyers get involved. You have two options. Either you can offer a draft of the contract which of course will be done in favor of you or the buyer can offer his draft. In the first option you have to invest time and money in your lawyers to prepare it. The lawyers unlike the M&A consultants charge by worked hours. In the second option you will reduce the initial cost but it will take you longer time to negotiate the draft because most probably it will be written in favor of the buyer. It is crucial that you "control" the lawyers so that you negotiate just the legal aspects of the deal not the structure. Sometimes, the lawyers, either because they want to play bigger role in the process or because they want to make money (they are paid buy hours as I said) they start to comment also stuff like the price of the deal, etc. This might open the Pandora box. Both parties in the deal (buyer and seller) have put significant efforts to agree on the deal and now when it has technically to be just finalized the whole process can be taken back two or three steps. That's why the idea of this stage is whatever you have agreed with the buyer to be put in a legal form. Noting more or nothing less.

Step 11. Signing of the deal

After the documents are ready at a certain day the two parties go to the notary office and sign the papers. There is a champagne and everybody is happy. You might need to take some extra technical steps such as setting up a shareholder meeting, changing the board of the directors, requesting the approve of some regulatory bodies but all these tasks are technical and will be responsibility mainly of your lawyers.

Step 12 Integration

An owner usually believes that once he had signed the documents and had received the money that everything is over. Now he can go on a long vocation. It is not like that. In order the deal to be successful it is important how the integration of the two companies will happen or how the new owner will take over of your business. It is likely that you might have agreed also on an earn-out scheme. This means that some of the payments of the price you will receive based on the financial results of the company in the next 1-2 years.

There might be a requirement that you as an owner has to secure the resigning of some key contracts with suppliers or lessor. Therefore, even if you signed the documents the work around the deal will continue some time for you. This is a very important stage and we have an additional chapter just on the integration of the business later on in the book. Of course if you have sold just a stake of the company to a financial investor this problem will not exist for you. But we have to describe all possible outcomes in the book.

Another key moment in the M&A process is who has more power in the process. The buyer or the seller. It depends on several factors and it doesn't have to be constant at all stages of the project. It will be good to know what the power balance is in any moment because it will determine your tactics in the process. One of the cases when the buyer can receive more power is when early in the process he submits a binding offer and set a deadline for its acceptance. When you sign an exclusivity agreement with a potential buyer he also receives more power. This agreement can be extended and this way the other interested parties to lose their interest completely. Even if it doesn't work out with the chosen buyer after 4-5 months the other potential investor would have started other projects and their enthusiasm for the deal will be completely different than the one in the beginning of the process. That's why you have to be careful when and with whom you sign an exclusivity agreement. In the beginning of the M&A process when the seller decides whom to contact and what information to provide to the various interested parties he is in the stronger position. Like in any game it will be good for you if you can "read the cards" so that you know in each moment how pushy you can be in the negotiations.

A long process like an M&A deal which has many stages and many unknowns is a complex topic but there are some rules which can be summarized and which can increase your chances to successfully close the deal. Here they are:
 You must have a clear goal what you want to achieve with this process. I have been a witness to deals where the owner receives a very good offer. We are talking for an offer of 8 figures in euro. For some reasons he doesn't proceed further to close the deal. After some time I asked him why he did that. He told me: "I just wanted to see how much they will give me for my business". Any M&A process requires a significant recourses in terms of money and time. If you as an owner are ready to invest just to receive an objective indication what the value of your business it is your right. However, it will be good to discuss it with your team at the very beginning of the process so that everybody is on the same page during the process.

 Transparency. As a continuation of the above example you as an owner has to be transparent during the whole process. Mainly not to cheat. Very often when you try to hide a fact it comes out later in the negotiations or in the due diligence process. Sometimes this can be fixed but the fact that you cheated or exaggerated will leave in the buyer the sense that he cannot trust you anymore for anything. The risk for him increases and he starts to doubt any piece of information you give him. In order to make sure that there will be no surprise and to "insure" himself he will discount the valuation or will put other protecting clauses in the contract. That's' why unless you are completely sure that a certain fact cannot be discovered during the whole process it will be better to reveal it in the beginning.

Communication. In general the lack of good communication is the cause for most of our problems not only in the professional but also in the personal life. Communicate often and clearly all issues during the whole process. A significant part of the family owned business are not prepared and when the buyer wants from them some information which according to the buyer should take 3 days you as an owner send it to him in two weeks. We have a problem. The buyer starts thinking that there is some hidden issues and that you are negotiating with somebody else behind his back. It will be better to tell him that you don't have the resources for his request and it will take you longer time to provide the requested info. Otherwise you will create wrong impression in him.

Set aside the necessary recourses. When you work with big companies who are potential buyers they have set aside in advance the necessary resources to buy companies. Sometimes they have internal M&A department which is what they do for living. To buy new companies. You on the other side there is no way to have such resources. Now your accountant besides the ordinary operating work also has to spend time to prepare various reports for the needs of the investors. If you have decided to go down the path of an M&A deal you have to put aside the required resources for that. Yes, the outside consultants can help you but you will need also internal resources. The most important one is your personal attention.

Despite the fact that an M&A process has many unknowns it will be good if you have some initial timeframe and to try to follow it as much as it is possible. You cannot control the other party. How much time they will need to discuss the offer in the board or how much time they will need to send a binding offer, However, you can control your actions. If you don't have such timeframe for the deal, the process will prolong further. The longer it takes for a deal to close the bigger the probability that it will not close at all.

If it is normal that an M&A process will take about a year and you don't have to take off your attention form the operating problems in the company. That's why it always helps to have a team of outside consultant which will concentrate on the M&A process while your focus during that time on the operating results of the company. Otherwise you financial results of the business will get worse and after you agreed on the deal terms it will turn out that the company profit is down 15%, You also used the profit as an anchor for the valuation. A red light will show up in the investors head. He will wonder what is happening and normally will try to renegotiate the price because now the financial results are lower. That's why keep a close eye on your operating results during the whole stages of the M&A process.

As you can see I described the typical steps for a bigger company which is organizing an auction process. If you have a small business like a restaurant or you have a trade partner who knows your business and makes you a surprising offer some of the steps will be dropped out. But now you are familiar with all stages so you are prepared. In the next chapters we will get into more details for some of the steps we discussed in this chapter.

Preparation of the Company for a Sell

Everyone will agree with the statement that the good preparation is a prerequisite for the success of an activity. Nevertheless if we are talking for a preparation for an exam, a competition, a presentation or the sale of a company and if you rely just on the improvisation there is a huge probability that something might goes wrong. Everybody knows how to prepare himself for an exam or for a presentation but how to prepare for the sale of a company. For some companies this step will take long time while for others it might not take so long. Actually we can accept that some companies are almost ready for an M&A process because that's the way how they are managed. With clear rules and independent processes. As the experts say: the companies have established corporate structures. During last years more and more family business are trying to build corporate structure in their organizations. Why is that important? There are two main advantages: The existence of a corporate structure allows the company to grow fast and to scale it business model. If they didn't build a corporate structure then the growth potential is limited to the growth potential of its owner. For example, on practice if you have one restaurant the business might be developing very well because you are every day in the restaurant and you keep a close eye on all processes. However, when you decide to grow your business because it is doing well and open 5-6 more restaurants you can see that the new restaurants are not doing as well as the first restaurant. The reason is that you cannot control them personally. If there are no clear written rules and procedures everybody is doing whatever he decides. The second reason is that if you haven't established such structure then the whole business is dependable on you. The investors don't like this fact at all and very often it is a big burden to close a deal successfully.

Companies which are managed in such way, not to be dependable on their owners, are prepared for an M&A process. These companies just need a little bit "polishing" and they can launch the process. The rest of the companies, if they want to close the deal successfully, will need several months in order to prepare for this step. Many of the family businesses in Bulgaria are not prepared for an M&A process and that's why we, in our team at Synergy Group, were "forced" to also perform some management consulting projects. Not only financial consulting which is our main focus as part of the process of mergers and acquisitions. Of course sometimes you can close a deal even without any preparation but in these case either the business is small (a restaurant for example) or the price which you will receive from the buyer is not the maximum which can be received. The risk for the potential buyer will be bigger and he will prefer to "protect" himself by offering a discounted valuation. We can divide the whole process of preparation into the following main major topics:

What makes your business attractive to the investors?
Setting up the sale team
Clearing up your financials
Preparation of the necessary documents
Coming up with your story

Let's discuss in more details each of these five topics

What makes your business attractive to the investors?

With the various companies and the different investors there might be some variations but there is a set of some basic characteristics which always make a good impression in any investor.

The possibility a company to operate independently of its owner. This issue we already discussed in the part of the corporate structure so I will not get into more details. There is a very easy test to check if your company have established a corporate structure. If you as an owner go to the Maldives for 2-3 months and when you come the business didn't worsen its financial results this means that you have managed to build clear rules and procedure for its operation. When you sell 100% of your company this is one of the most important characteristics for the new owner.

Financial indicators. Whatever we discuss we know that a business is created and exists to bring financial dividends to its owners. That's why the financial results of your company are of significant importance. Here we can have four situations: In the first situation your company has increasing revenues and profits. This is the dream case. Any investor would be attracted by such company and this puts you in a very strong position in the M&A process. In the second case you have increasing sales but decreasing or stable profits. Here the potential buyer might have some concerns and to ask himself if the expenses related to the sale of your products are out of control. Actually in that situation there is no point to grow your business. I guess some of you have been in a situation when they had 20 employees and were making 100 000 euros net profit. After several years the business grew and you had three times more employees and increased your sales three times but you were still making 100 000 euros net profit. Then you started asking yourself what was wrong. Why did you have to put all this additional efforts and stress when you made the same profit with a small team of 20 people. Another concern which the potential buyer can have is whether company expenses in general are out of control. This is not a fatal problem but for sure the investor will be concerned and he would like to find out the reason for this discrepancy in advance. That will happen before he makes an offer. In most cases the problem can be fixed but it has to be done by the new owner and that's why most probably he will discount his offer because he will have additional work to do. If you as an owner identify the reason for that problem and start working on it will be of benefit for your valuation and attractiveness

. In the third situation your company can have decreasing sales but with stable level of the net profit. This is also not a perfect situation because here comes the question: How long this trend of decreasing sales will continue and can it stop at all? What are the reasons for that? Perhaps the industry itself is in such phase that the consumers have found an alternatives to your product or there are many competitors in the field and the industry is not growing anymore. This means that there will be a redistribution of market shares among the participants because the pie is not increasing anymore. For sure the potential buyer will have some concerns in this situation too. The fourth case is when you have decreasing sales and a loss from your activities. Here things can become very complex. Everybody is aware that your business has some difficulties and the company sale will be a very hard task. It is not clear if there is still business left or the only things which has any worth is just the assets. If you are in such situation usually means that you sell your business because you got into an extreme situation. For example they have health problems or they recovered the business from inheritance and don't know what to do with it. It can be just a temporary situation. Many good companies for some years had financial difficulties and had decreasing sales and financial losses. The key here is to see if there is a trend and this continues 3-4 years or it is just temporally. It can also be the result of outside objective reason like a world financial crisis. Don't worry too much for that situation. There is a saying that there are passengers for each train so you can also find a buyer for troubled businesses. The question is what the terms will be. In general if you have decided to sell your business it will be good to "polish" it a little bit. Everybody knows that when you are going to an auto shop for used cars the cars there are shiny and polished and they look very attractive although they are second hand. Despite the short time you will have, the specifics of the industry and your business allows you must try to decrease some of the expenses and increase a little bit the sales. This will have an impact on your financial statements and it will look good in the eyes of the potential buyers.

Clients' diversification. Nobody likes businesses which depends on 2-3 big clients. I came across companies where over 50% of the revenues comes from one client. For example many furniture companies work mainly for Ikea. That fact is not preferred by the investors because the risk for them will be too big if Ikea, for whatever reason, decides to give up and find a replacement to your product. Yes, it can be perceived that such contracts give you security and predictability but nobody likes to be dependable only on one person or company. This doesn't mean that you cannot sell your business but now we are talking for factors which make your company more attractive to the investors. The concentration of your sales into few key clients doesn't make your business attractive to the buyers.

Well-kept business. This is hard to explain and I have difficulties to find the right phrase. Just imagine an apartment. A person can say right away from the moment he enters that the apartment was well-kept by the owner and what was his attitude to the small details. Now I recall a situation where I took a foreign fund manager to a Bulgarian company for a visit. He told me that in such visits he also pay attention to the condition of the company toilets. By their condition you can judge what the attitude of the owner towards his employees is. In this group of factors we can also include other items which might look minor at first sight but they reveals if your apartment, i.e. your business is well-kept. For example your company web site, your office and even your e-mails. A lot of owners have businesses that make 1-2 million profit per year but their e-mail is in Gmail or in Yahoo. It doesn't look professional. Nowadays it will cost you literally 50-100 euros to have own company e-mails.

Unique product or services. If you have a product or a service which stands out from the ones of your competitors then for sure you will have a competitive advantage. It will have an impact on your company financial results but it will also make an impression to the investors. You have to look at this item in more general view. I am not talking just for technological products. For example if you are in the retail business the most important component for your business is the location. So if you managed to open a store at a top location then you have for sure a unique product.

Modern buildings and equipment. If you invest consistently in your business and your equipment is up to date with the most modern machines then the potential buyers will be impressed. This fact shows them that next years they don't have to make a lot of capital expenditures and with the current equipment they will be able to keep the current profitability the next 4-5 years. If your machines and equipment are outdated you might be making 1 mill net profit and based on that to expect 10 mill euros valuation but it will not happen. The reason is that you cannot keep your profit 1 mill euros (other factors constant) for the next 3-4 years with the current old equipment. If you want to keep that profitability you would have to buy new machines and this will increase the investment of the buyer. If you remember two of the deal cases I gave you in the beginning of the books the owners had just built new factories before selling the companies to foreign investors.

Great team. Every business depends to much bigger extend on its team than on and its machines. If you have managed to create a great team of loyal employees who feel pride and pleasure to work for your company it will impress the potential buyers. It is not a coincidence that the investors very often ask for the age structure of your employees, their education and how long they have been with the company. They want to know how hard is to find new employees, etc.

Entry barriers. If you operate in an industry which has high barriers for the entrance of new players that would be considered an advantage. These barriers can be from a technological nature or just consumer habits which will take time to be changed. Another option is that your industry require licenses to operate as a business in it. In this case you are in the mercy of the government or other regulatory institutions. For example you might want to open a new bank or to set a lottery business or to search for gold. Well, you cannot do it by yourself without the permission of a regulatory body. This is called high barrier of entry for new players. If you are in such situation it will make your business more attractive.

The stage of development of the industry. It really matters if your industry is growing or declining and if the profit margins are high or low. For example the profit margins of the IT companies are very different than the ones in the food manufacturers. One of the key issue here is that industries which rely on the low labor cost in order to survive are not attractive to the buyers. Long years Bulgaria and Eastern Europe positioned itself as a place with low cost employees and that's how we attracted foreign investors. That's OK but we also wanted our salaries to reach the level of the salaries in Western Europe. This is happening as a trend and as a result the companies which relied on the cheap labor in Eastern Europe are having now difficulties. A good example is the sewing industry. In the 90s that industry developed very fast in Bulgaria and we had a lot of companies. Now the salaries went up and the Bulgarian companies are not competitive anymore. Many of them went bankrupt. This is one of the reasons why we don't have almost any M&A deals in that sector in Bulgaria. No investor wants to invest in companies which don't have own product and work just to order with an increasing labor cost in the product structure. If you have a brand it will be a different story but without brand the probability to have an interested buyer is minimal.

Low capital expenditures (CAPEX). There are some industries which require very high CAPEX for the update of their equipment. For example the cement industry and the glassware industry. If you are in such industry the investors will not be excited and usually the multiples which they will offer for your valuation, which will discuss later on in the book, will be smaller than that in the other industries. They just have to make significant CAPEX on every 4-5 years.

Transferability of the business. Here the issues are in some way related to building the corporate structure in the company. However it is not only the issue with the transferability of the ownership of the company. We also include in this group how easy it is to transfer the clients and even business contracts. Some of the contracts can have clauses which say that the contracts become void or on demand if there is a change in the ownership of the company. The banks all the time do it with the bank credits. Another example is that if you have rents for the stores then the contract can become void if there is a change in the ownership of the retail chain and it is not approved by the owner of the stores.

Cleaning the balance sheet of the company

This topic is a natural extension of the issue with the financial results of a company and what an owner has to do in order to improve its financial results just before the deal. However it also has another important characteristic. Very often the family owned business don't think about the process of an eventual company sale and since it is their own business they mix their personal assets with those owned by the business. As a result in a sunny day it turns out that their personal house in practice is owned by their company. Their personal car also is in the balance sheet of the company. There might be also assets which are used by other businesses but owned by the company which is for sale. All this cases might lead to problems when you are trying to determine what the valuation of the company is. You as an owner know what assets there are in the balance sheet of the company but for the potential buyers these assets are of no interest since they don't contribute to the sales and to the net profit of the company. That's why your accountants and lawyers have to clean up the company balance sheet of assets which don't contribute to the financial results. Once you do it your company will be ready for the M&A process. You also can improve the effectiveness of your financial ratio by trying to collect bigger part of your account receivables. This step will also increase the cash in the company and usually the available cash in a company is paid off by the buyers or it is distributed to the current owners. These actions will also improve some key financial indicators which are followed by the financial analysts when they make a valuation of your company. You can also check your inventory. How much of it is really available in the warehouses and how much is there just on paper.

How much of the inventory actually can be sold? We had cases when a company had a lot of goods and raw materials according to the accounting documents and this increased the assets value in the balance sheet. A significant part of the inventory however was available just on paper or was useless in practice for the business. So in reality the money which standed behind them were just fraction from their balance number. It will be good if you this this checkup in advance. Otherwise you might mislead the potential buyers with the data. Most probably he will find out when he starts the due diligence process but he might believe that you wanted to cheat him and that you had done it on purpose. The whole process of transferring assets and cleaning out the balance sheet will require you to make additional expenses which the owners don't want to do and that's why they delay it. However, at some point you have to tide up your house and it will be better if you do it in advance. Not after you have negotiated the term sheet and then the due diligence shows that there are discrepancies in the numbers you have provided to the investors.

Create your team which will handle the M&A process

Very often the company owners are trying to handle the whole process by themselves. I, as an M&A consultant with 15 years experience in the field, will be subjective in my opinion. I have a personal interest to convince you that you cannot do it without a professional consultant. However, I will try to present you some facts objectively on the topic and you can decide by yourself if you can do it alone or you will need some help. The smaller is your business the less complex the potential transaction will be and there is a bigger chance that you can handle it successfully just by yourself. I believe that the role of the consultant is mainly into two directions: First, the whole process of selling a company takes a lot of time and resources and either you and your team has to set aside time for that task or you have to hire outside people. Since I have also developed two my own startups (I have described that experience in another book) to the addition to my work as an M&A consultant I recall the following case. The two projects were in the field of educational technology.

We have developed our own software for a virtual classroom. Something like Zoom. There was a discussion among our potential clients that it is it better for them to take an open source product which in its nature is free or to use a SaaS product. In the SaaS product you pay for it and you don't have to worry about anything else. In the so called free open source software you must have your own servers and system administrators who will set them up and manage them. You also have to take care of all customer problems. All this stuff cost money but the clients don't think about them because they believe that the open source software is free. I remember that one of the first lessons I learned in the university about 25 years ago is that there is no free lunch. That will be the case also with you as an owner. The time which you have to invest in the process will be from your personal time and that of your employees. Even if you don't calculate it officially it will not be for free. The second reason to form such team is that the M&A consultant do this task every day. The mergers and acquisitions as a process is not rocket science but it is like that with most activities. If I have to bake bread and pastries most probably after several months I will be very good at that. The issue is that I don't do it every day and that's why most probably I will make worse pastries than most people who do it for living. Most probably all of you will agree with these two advantages of having a professional M&A consultant in your team. The problem is in the fees which you have to pay them. When you sell a company in most cases the deal is much bigger in value than is the sale of a house for example. As a result the fees in absolute amounts are also much bigger in the

M&A deals and they will poke your eyes. If a company is sold for 5 mill euros then it is normal that the consultant will receive around 150 000 as a success fee which is not a small number.

My advice is not to look at the fees in absolute amounts but as an added value for you from that fees. If your consultant manage to sell your company for 5 500 000 euros instead of 5 00 000 euros then you will have a return of the investment of more than 300 000 euros from your decision to hire an M&A consultant. This makes around 200% return. Not a bad return at all, right? The bad part of that exercise is that this is not math and it is very hard to forecast that it will happen exactly like that. These big fees in absolute amounts which are perceived as the remuneration of the M&A consultants lead to another problem. It is very tempting for a lot of people to act as M&A consultants and many people like lawyers, real estate brokers, etc are trying to be M&A consultants. They think that the job of the M&A consultant is to connect John and Smith and for that he will receive a lucrative success fee. In other words they think that M&A consultants are brokers. Because of that wrong perception it is even more crucial to choose the right M&A team. Before I give you some tips what to look for when you are choosing your M&A team let me first explain why I am talking for a team. Depending on your business, how big and complex it is, you will need: a financial or an M&A consultant, a lawyer who is specialized in the M&A deals not just commercial law or even worse divorce lawyer, an appraiser which can do the valuation of the company but this step can also be done by the M&A consultant, and an accountant who in most cases can be somebody from your accounting department. Here are the factors to which to pay attention to when you are choosing your M&A team:

Look for a consultant, not for a broker. That's why it is very important that he is aware from the very beginning that he will work just for you and will protect your interests. He is not supposed to act as a broker and to expect commission form both parties in a deal. In the USA there are different names for that type of people and for real some of them are called brokers. Others are called investment bankers. In essence there is no difference in their work it just depends how big deal they are working on. The brokers work on smaller deals and the investments bankers work on bigger transactions. There is a small difference also in their remuneration. The brokers are usually taking a bigger percent as a success fee because their work is not much different than that of the investment bankers in terms of efforts. They just have to work on a deal for 1 mill euros instead of 15 mill euros. In general I call both groups M&A consultant so that I can distinguish them from the real estate brokers.

It will be good if these people have experience and track record in doing deals in the field of mergers and acquisitions. If they have done deals in your industry it will be even better because they will have some initial knowledge about the industry and the main players in it. That's why in the USA the team usually specialize in sectors. In small countries like Bulgaria it is hard to specialize because the market is very small and it is very hard for a consultant to do deals just in the energy sector for example. As in any other profession you should check the deals which these people have done and what is the outcome. Don't rely on their words that they know a lot of people. You don't want a broker. Nowadays the added value is not to know that Coca-Cola might be interested to buy your business. Everybody can get into Google and make a list of the biggest players in your industry and present it as a list of potential buyers.

You want a consultant who feels confident in his skills and knowledge and knows what he is doing. You will feel it from the conversations you will have with him. The consultant doesn't have to be arrogant just confident. The confidence come from the deals which he had done.

You have to match with that person. People have different personalities. You will work very closely with that person for about a year and that's why it is important to "click" together.

You would like to have a person who also plays the role of an independent advisor. In order this to happen you have to structure his remuneration in such way that the consultant doesn't try to convince you to close any type of deal just because he also has to eat something. That's why in Western Europe and also lately in Eastern Europe the M&A consultant don't' anymore work just on a success fee. This is a percent of the deal amount which the consultant receives if the deal is signed. There are various fixed fees which can be structured in different ways but now I will not get into details in that topic. In general these additional fixed fees are called retainers. Your consultant, if he is experienced, will know what structure to offer you so that it best works for your case.

 The consultant has to be creative and to have good communication and presentation skills. It doesn't matter how much financial analysis has to be made. In the end the decisions are taken by people not computers. The personal impression which your team leaves in the eyes of the investor will be crucial for his decisions. However, let's not forget that the investor is buying your business and it doesn't matter how charming the consultant is if the company owner acts unprofessionally then he can ruin all efforts.

 Whether to hire a boutique company like Synergy Group or to hire a big name player like KPMG, Deloitte, etc depends on the situation in which you are and what your goal is. Both options have their advantages. I can write a whole chapter on the topic. In a nutshell it is normal the big players to be more expensive and if you have comparatively small company there will be no point to hire and you cannot afford big names as a consultant. Why the big names are more expensive is a long topic and I don't want to open now the Pandora box. For sure the name of the consultant install trust in the potential buyers and if you have a big name as a consultant you might attract more potential buyers and perhaps better offers. These consultant know what they are doing and have a lot of resources. My experience reveals that in most cases the company owners choose a big name consultant for the following reasons: If you are the CEO of a big international company which had decided to sell its operations in Bulgaria then the board will have the choice to hire a big name company or a local M&A boutique company. If you hire a boutique company and the deal is closed successfully the CEO will save a lot of money but his award will be just a tap on his shoulder for the good work. If the local consultant screws up and the deal fails then the CEO is going home for sure.

That's why the CEOs all over the world prefer to work with big names companies. Just to "insure" themselves in case the deal fails. If something goes wrong the CEO can say: "Merrill Lynch advised us to act like this" and he is safe. If Synergy Group advised you on this plan the CEO will have a problem. Now I recall how many times our prime minister tells us that a certain decision is good because it was recommended by the International Monetary Fund. However, he doesn't tell how many times IMF screwed up in a lot of countries. Or how many cases we have when some of the big names have audited the financials of some companies (I can just mention Enron) and the result was devastating. Sometimes the big auditors pay a huge fine and continue. That's why you as an owner have to think very carefully what expenses you can afford for this task, how prepared you are to take a risk with a boutique consultant, and the most important thing is who actually will advise you on the deal. You might sign a deal with Merrill Lynch but the whole deal to be run mainly by a 25-30 years old guys. The senior partner who "sold" you the deal will show up from time to time.

Who is actually doing the deal for you? Merrill Lynch or the 30 years old guy?

Here comes the question where to find that consultant from? The most natural way is through referrals. Very often the company owners are worried to ask for such referrals because it will become clear right away that they are planning to sell their company. As we talked in the beginning of the book this is a huge problem. That's why in 21st century your best assistant will be Google. Read some information and feedbacks for the companies which are active in the M&A sector. Meet with some of them and then you can take a decision based on your gut and information you have gathered. At this stage you can also ask a friend for advice for a specific firm. After you choose your M&A consultant you also have to choose a lawyer. Either you can repeat the whole process again or your M&A consultant can recommend you a lawyer with whom he is working with. The big companies can offer you a full service and this is one of their advantages.

Preparation of the documents for the M&A process

Before you start contacting potential buyer you must prepare three documents. They can be prepared by your M&A consultant if you hired one or by yourself. There is also a third option but it applies mainly for the big companies. Since they make a lot of acquisitions that type of companies have internal M&A departments which are doing that as main activity. Since the book is mainly focused on the family business they usually don't have such departments. Actually I know a couple Bulgarian big holdings which are family businesses but they are more the exception than the rule. Anyway, it doesn't matter so much. The key point is that you must have these three documents in order to run a professional process.

The first document which we mentioned earlier in the book is the short anonymous presentation and it is called a Teaser. Within 1-2 pages you have to summarize the key facts of the company and the main characteristics of the proposed deal.

The second document is the Information memorandum of the company. It can vary from 15-20 PowerPoint slides to a 100 pages word document. This document is very important because based on it and the information inside the potential buyer will decide if it is worth the time to come and meet you to discuss the details of the deal. Sometimes the process is structured in such way that the buyers might be required even to submit an indicative non-binding offers just based on the Information memorandum. If you have a smaller business the buyer most probably will be a local player and you can get away with just 15-20 pages PowerPoint presentation. Now I am discussing the standards cases we have worked on and these are bigger Bulgarian companies which are sold to foreign investors. How exactly to prepare this IM is a technical work and your consultant will know his job but just for your information here are the main topics which have to be included in the document.

Information about the economic situation in your local country and the macroeconomic key indicators. Not all investors will be familiar with the business environment in your country. For example I am still surprised that only few foreign investors know that Bulgaria has only 10%

corporate tax although our government and all institution proclaim this fact for already 10 years.

Information about the industry in which the company operates in. What are the trends? What is expected as new regulations or development of the technology? How these changes will impact the business of the companies in that industry?

A short description of the history of the company. The major milestones. Also information about the shareholder structure.

A description of the product and services which you company is offering to its clients

What are the assets of the company such as buildings, machines, trucks, etc.?

The organizational structure of the company and information about the employees you have. A detail report on their age, qualification, how long they have been with the company, etc.

Information about the market and your competitors

Information about your Intellectual property, your patents, brands, trademarks, and the software products you own. In general all non-fixed assets you have.

Financial information. Here you have to include a balance sheet and an income statement for the last three years. You can also add a cash flow report. Financial analysis of the three documents and calculation of some key financial ratios.

Description of the investments which the company has made in the last 4-5 years.

A short plan and forecast for the development of the company for the next three years.

The third documents which has to be prepared by you or your consultant is the valuation report of the company. There are several methods how to do a valuation of a company but since we will have a separate chapter only on that topic I will discuss them there. This valuation report cannot be mandatory for any buyer but it will give an indication why your demands are reasonable and what are the reasons behind for asking that price.

Tell your story

The last 5th part of the preparation process is probably the most important one – your story. You know that nowadays the best presentations are based on the storytelling. People don't want to hear facts and data but they are impressed by the story which you can tell them. Your story will start with an answer of the question why are you selling. But it also must include your plans as a person and also the plans for the development of the company. This story is even more important when you are selling just a stake of your business and you want to attract an investment fund as a partner. Some of the entrepreneurs don't have a story or actually are ready to tell different versions as long as they can get rid of their business. This is OK in general but it is not Ok to say when the investor ask you in the middle of the process: "What do you want?" and your answer to be: "I want to sell a stake in the business but if you want 100% of the company there is no problem".

Actually you can have a good story when you are sincere. However, you know that telling 100% of the truth not always is good for you. I guess there is no guy who tells his wife 100% of everything but the closer it is to the truth it sounds more logical and convincing. The most important is that you are not caught also in a lie. That's why if you are really tired of developing the business just admit it. This is not something bad. It is also not a problem to have a couple stories. To one type of buyers you can tell one story and to another group of buyers to tell a different story. You can tell a strategic buyer that you want just to retire while you can tell an investment fund that you want a partner and together to take over the world. This is not impossible as a strategy but you have to be very careful in the negotiations. Everything in the deal will change with the different stories. From the structure of the deal to what will happen after the deal. That's why you as an owner has to think very well what to do and what you want to achieve with the launch of an M&A process. It must be based on your goals and to build one coherent story. It might sound funny to you but practice this story as many times as necessary while you start believing in it on 100%.

There are many issues which we didn't discuss and specific steps which you can take to increase the attractiveness of your business. You cannot say for sure when this stage of the preparation for your company ends. As you saw some of the steps have to take place before the process but some of the actions will continue even during the negotiations with the buyers. My goal was to show you how important is this stage in the whole M&A process and how actually most of the work has to be done before you start calling the investors. On the other side this doesn't have to make you postpone the process indefinitely with the excuse that your company is not ready to be sold. There is no company which is ready on 100%. There are also outside factors which have a huge impact on your deal. For example the M&A market is very hot or a competitor is acquired by an aggressive financial investor. An investor might have aggressive strategy for consolidation and he has to make several acquisitions within 2-3 years before he exit the investment. That's why you have to run your company in such way that it is prepared for a sale in any moment of its existence. This will help you also with improving the operating results.

Buyers of your business

It doesn't matter how well prepared you are if there are no interested buyers. There will be no deal in that case. The key question is which can be the organizations or the people who can buy your company or at least a stake from it? We can divide them into individual investors and institutional investors. They can also be different parties depending on the fact if you are selling assets or your business. In general the most common division of the potential buyers is into strategic investors and financial investors. Last years the boundary between the two groups blur a little bit because many of the financial investors own big companies and they make many add-on acquisitions through these companies. For example one of the biggest factories in Bulgaria is Ideal Standard which produces bathroom equipment. If they decide to buy your company you will say that the buyer was a strategic player. On the other side Ideal Standard is owned already by a big investment fund so you can say that actually the buyer of your business is a financial player.

The financial investors themselves can be divided into three and even four subgroups with their specific characteristics. Besides these two groups of buyer there are also several other options. They might not be so popular but you as an owner still can sell your business to one of them. I will stop and explain each group of potential buyers with short description of its characteristics. Depending on your goals and the specifics of your company you can decide which group of potential buyers is the most appropriate for you. We will start first with the financial players:

Private Equity Funds

This is the most popular type of a financial buyer. What are they? How are they working and what type of private equity funds do we have? The goal of any private equity fund is to find interesting companies which to invest in, to develop their business, and in several years to exit the company with a good profit. So basically the main goal of the fund is to make a good return on their investment. In order this process to happen the first step is a group of experts (the management team) has to raise capital from some organizations. In most cases the team is comprised of financiers. Sometimes you can have people who used to work in specific industries especially if the sector is one of the priority ones for the fund. In general you cannot expect that the management of the fund will be big experts in the activities of your company. I am sure that you know that there are a lot of available money in the world. In the last 12 years, after the financial crisis from 2008, the governments printed a lot of cash as an anti-crisis measure. These money has to go somewhere. They are invested in various assets. You can invest them in government bonds, shares on the stock exchange, real estate and some riskier investments. One of those riskier investments is exactly buying of an active business.

It doesn't matter how profitable a company looks at the moment there is no guarantee that in 4-5 years it won't go bankrupt and disappear as a business. It can happen for objective and subjective reasons. In Bulgaria we have several such examples for companies which had turnover of over 50 mill euros which are considered big size companies here. I am sure that you can come up with such examples in your own country. In the USA I can recall right away companies like K-mart, Radioshack, etc. Since the investment is risky in its essence, the expected yield from such investments is 15-20% on an annual base. If the managers cannot make such return from investing in businesses the funds will change their investment strategy and to switch to less riskier investments like buying office building or shopping malls. Pretty much this small team of financial guys (the fund management) goes to the big institutional investors such as insurance companies or pension funds, private investors, banks, etc. and tell them: "We are very good managers and we have a plan in what undervalued companies to invest in. If you give us some money for management we can make a good profit for you". It is not easy at all to convince the big players in the world to trust you with their money. Especially when they have to give you tens of million dollars and you are raising capital for your first fund. That's why in Eastern Europe very often as investors in such funds participate public institutions such as the European Investment Fund or the European Bank for Reconstructuring and Development (EBRD). The management team also has to participate with some personal money but usually it is a very small part of the whole capital. It is usually 3-10% of the whole capital of the fund. In general these people are managing other people's money. Once they raise the funds the management team has to identify companies with potential, to buy a stake in them, to develop them and make them bigger and more profitable.

After several years to sell them to another investor and with the proceeds to return the money to the insurance companies and the pension funds. All these steps have to take place in most cases within ten years. That's why we can say that with that type of buyers their perspective is short-term or actually more of mid-term timeframe. In the ideal case for the funds is to sell your company within 3-4 years after they had invested in it. This time restrictions sometimes can have advantages and sometimes disadvantages for you as an entrepreneur. If the fund is close to the end of their investment period (the time during which they can make investments in new companies) and they still have a lot of available funds the fund team will be forced to make investments very quickly. They will have to move very fast and most probably you will be able to negotiate better terms on the deal. And vice versa. If the end if the life of the fund is approaching the fund can make you sell the company even if the company is not in its best condition or the M&A market is not so favorable. Why all these stuff concerns you as an owner. Because in most cased the private equity funds will not buy the whole company but they will buy a stake in it. Since these guys are not experts in the sector but financial guys, they prefer if you continue to "drive the car".

They will try to be your navigator so that the car can reach the end destination much faster with their help. We can say that that type of investors will be appropriate for you if you want to expand your business quickly, need a partner, and they can be of help with that plan. There are also cases when a PE Fund can buy the whole company but this is much rare as an occasion. If they already have an investment in the same sector then the fund can do it because it already can use the operating management from their current investment. In regards to that we can say that a PE fund in theory can buy 100% of your business, a majority stake, or a minority stake. When the fund management goes to its investors to raise capital it has a business strategy in advance. How big stake they will acquire in the companies, in what sectors and in what countries. After they receive the money they have to follow this strategy and cannot change the parameters of the investments. The fund also has the option to make cash out deals or to invest money in the company for growth. In the first option you sell for example 60% of the business for 6 mill and these money goes into your personal bank account. You can do whatever you want with them. This is what most entrepreneurs want but this sit not the preferred option by the fund managers. The second option is if your company valuation is 10 mill they will acquire 60% for around 6 mill euros but the money will stay in the company and will be used for its future development. Another characteristics is that for the management of the fund capital the fund managers receive every year some money which they use for due diligence of the companies they will invest in and also to cover the expenses of the managers (salaries, offices, etc). In most cases it is 2-3% of the amount of the managed funds on an annual base. That's why the fund managers have the internal desire to manage bigger and bigger funds. This way they will receive more money for the management of the fund. As you can assume the amount of work and efforts for a company which has a valuation of 5 mill and 20 mill is pretty much the same. That's why these funds prefer to make bigger investments. From an objective point of view if you manage a 100 mill euros fund and you make an investment of around 5 mill euros per company then you will have around 20 companies in your portfolio. It is clear that the fund team will not manage on an operating level these companies but it will be hard for them even to go just to the monthly board meetings.

That's why the find teams want to make bigger investment and as a result not many companies in small countries like Bulgaria are appropriate targets for such investors. About 10 years ago we had perhaps around 10 PE funds which operated and made investments in Bulgaria. Gradually they disappeared one by one. Afterwards the European investment fund created two local funds which made around 10-15 investments but they also run out of capital. Now several other funds are prepared to be launched but in general we don't have many funds which can do investments in smaller Bulgarian companies. We are talking for deals under 10 mill euros per company. Otherwise in a world scale if you are talking for investments of over 10-15 mill euros there are a lot of PE funds and you can have a big choice of such potential buyers. The most important thing which you have to remember for the PE funds is that they invest only in business, not in assets. Because of that if your company is not in a good financial situation the fund will have no interest in it nevertheless what the prices is.

Venture capital Funds

That type of buyers are very similar to the private equity funds with some minor differences. They usually invest smaller amounts in younger companies which have the potential for a significant growth. For the VC funds will be a big exception to buy a 100% of the company. For sure they will insist that the investment they make to stay in the company. So there will be no cash out and the money will be used to develop the company further. In most cases we can talk mostly for technological businesses. In general the way of creation and function of the VC funds is similar to that of the PE funds. Perhaps the clearers criteria for the separation between the two types of funds is the stage in which they invest in a certain company.

Family Offices.

This form of investors is no very common in Eastern Europe but it is getting more popularity in the world. These investors can invest in companies from various countries and this way you as an owner can bump into them even though they don't exist in your home country. In their essence they are also a financial investor but the sources of their capital usually comes from only one organization. It is a big family business/holding and that's where their name comes from. If you are part of such big family and have a very profitable business then you will generate significant amounts of free cash. You will wonder what to do with these money. Either because you want to diversify your family business or just because your current business doesn't need so much new investments you decide to set up an investment fund which can invest in other businesses. This fund will be managed either by the family or by outside managers. The key specific trait of the Family offices is that their investment horizon is much bigger and they are not pressed to exit their investments as the PE and VC funds are. In regards to that trait they are more similar to the strategic players. If you ask them how many years they are planning to keep their investment in the company they might tell you: "Forever". Because of that it is more likely the Family office to buy 100% of your business or the money which they invest in the company to be in the form of cash out. You as an owner can take the money and go to the Hawaii.

Mezzanine funds

I was wondering if I should include them in the group of the financial buyers because in their core they are more of a financing organization. However there is an option that they can also acquire a stake in your company and that's why I decided to include them here and to say a few words about the mezzanine funds. Their financing is a hybrid between the bank financing and the equity financing which provide the other three types of financial buyers. Imagine that you have a very fast growing business which needs a lot of cash in order to grow or makes a lot of acquisitions. The first thing which you can do as an owner is to look for bank financing since it is the cheapest form of financing for any business. Very often the banks have some rules, either internal or applied by the central banks, that they cannot give you more financing above some level. In most cases they calculate it as a multiple of EBITDA. If you are in such situation and don't want to sell a big chunk of your company to the PE funds then you can talk to the Mezzanine funds. In the mezzanine financing the price of the financing is a combination of an interest rate, like in the credits, and also some premium which has to be paid under some circumstances. The Mezzanine fund also have the opportunity to convert some part of that financing into a small stake in your company. In Bulgaria we have several examples of companies and deals which used that form of financing like Jet Credit or Eurohold. Now we also have a brand new Mezzanine fund which was set up with money from the European Investment Fund.

Strategic buyers

The term strategic players is actually a nice word for corporate buyers or these are other companies from the same sector you operate in. In this group we can see a variety of investors but what keeps them under the same denominator is that they are all long term investors. When they buy your business they do it with the idea that it is forever because there is some synergy with their main business. A person doesn't know how things will develop in 10 years and we have witnessed enough deals where strategic players sell some of their divisions or subsidiaries but they are not pressed for time. It is supposed that the reasons behind their decision to buy a company or not are not of financial nature. This doesn't mean that they don't negotiate hard like the PE funds and wants to do a good deal. However, you might be able to manage to sign a better deal because the strategic buyers are mot chasing 15-20% annual yield from their investments like most financial buyers. When together with your M&A consultant you are preparing the initial list of potential buyers your first reaction will be to include your direct competitors in that list. If you have a cosmetics manufacturing company it will be normal to include all cosmetics producers. However you don't have to limit yourself just to the direct competitors. You can also include companies which are your suppliers or clients. Pretty much think along the vertical integration axes. For example a retail store chain can also buy the manufacturer of the goods which it sells with the idea to close the whole cycle. That's why when you think for strategic buyers think in broader terms. I even would look around for companies which have several business divisions. For example manufacturing several groups of goods. If they have more than one group of products in their portfolio they can decide to expand it with another product. For example if the company is already producing salami it can decide also to start producing dairy products so that it make use of its very good distribution network with which it is famous for. That's why in the "B list" with potential buyers I would increase the possible range of potential strategic buyers. Since they are not financial players, the strategic buyer use different techniques when they close M&A deals. Here we can talk also about the possibility a strategic buyer to buy different assets, not only the whole business, which is impossible to happen with the financial buyers. There is no problem for them to buy 100% of your company but it is also possible that they will buy just a stake like a PE fund.

In most cases they use this approach of buying just a stake when the strategic buyers want to enter the market gradually because it is unknown for them. However almost always there is a clause form the very beginning that they will have options to increase their stake to 100% in the acquired business based on some predetermined criteria.

We have similar case with the Bulgaria courier company Speedy and the French DPD. A significant part of the Bulgarian entrepreneurs are dreaming to sell their business to strategic foreign investor. This is for them the perfect deal. Yes, it is true but we have to be aware that it is not so easy to happen. Bulgaria as most Eastern European countries are small markets. The companies are not so big and we have a problem with the size of the companies here. We can have a leader on the market and at the same time they have sales of around 10 mill euros. This is nothing in terms of the European standards and creates difficulties to attract foreign strategic buyers unless they are already present on the local market. Some time ago a foreign strategic investor wanted to buy a food retail chain in Bulgaria. Their condition was that the deal with the target company had to be at least for 30 mill euros and the target to be a top 5 player. As you can see it is not something unusual as requirements. Based on this criteria there was only one Bulgarian company which met these requirements and the owner was not interested in such talks. As a result the case was closed. No more options. For the foreign companies in Bulgaria it is a little bit different because the decisions are taken in their HQ. That's why if you are the owner of a comparatively small company according to the European standards the most probable buyers for your company will be local players. A good approach will be to do consolidation on the local market and then you can attract the big strategic players. To do such consolidation is very a hard step for the family business owners. I understand the Bulgarian entrepreneurs because it is much easier for them to reveal their financials and operations to players who are not present on the local market compared to offering their local competitor to buy them. You as an owner have to find the balance between the more opportunities and the confidentiality issue but my advice to you will be not to exclude the local strategic players especially if you are in a small market.

Selling on the stock exchange or IPO

When a company is doing an IPO on the stock exchange usually the owner will receive the best possible price in terms of valuation. Besides he will not have another big shareholder in the company structure which might try to run the show as the PE funds wants to do sometimes. It looks like the perfect option for finding an investor. In this case we also talk exclusively only for companies which have good financials and for the sale of business, not assets. In most cases you are selling a minority stake and it can be in the form of selling existing shares or increasing the capital by issuing new shares. It might be also combination of both options. This form allows you to cash out some of the efforts in your business which is very important to most company owners. In Bulgaria we had several deals on the Bulgarian stock exchange. Some of them before the financial crisis of 2008 and some after the crisis. In general the Bulgarian stock exchange is not a very good place for IPOs but it is a long story. There are a lot of objective reasons for this situation which have been discussed in the media but for me a huge fault for the current status of the stock exchange also have the Bulgarian entrepreneurs. What do I mean? Unfortunately we have a few cases in Bulgaria where the company owner decides to cash out a little bit from his business and he tries to sell 15-20% of the company on the stock exchange. The initial price is very often very high and right after the trading starts it goes down.

Perhaps it is not correct to say that price was high since the investors thought that it is worth it and bought the shares but it is a fact that in most cases after the trade starts the share prices go down. A lot of the minority shareholders are complaining that the majority shareholder doesn't treat them fairly and doesn't inform them about the plans for the development of the company. Usually the majority shareholder accepts the small investors as cash cows to get money out of them or for some idiots which cannot do any harm for him and are only source of cash. Their percentage in the company is so small that they cannot have any impact on the management of the company. In order to get out of this vicious cycle a Bulgarian entrepreneur would have to offer at least 60% of the capital for the IPO on the stock exchange. It is a majority stake but because of the many small investors most probably he will be able to manage the company with no problem even with just 40% of the capital. There are so many examples in the world where the main shareholder can manage effectively the company although he owns only 20-25% of the shares. However if he starts to treat the minority shareholders unfair they can consolidate themselves very fast and to take over the management of the company because cumulatively they own 60% of the firm. In Bulgaria we had one such case with one of the former privatization fund which was taken over by a local entrepreneur. However the company had a free float of 60%. Perhaps because of that case I haven't seen any more a Bulgarian company which is doing an IPO on the Bulgarian stock exchange to offer a majority stake. The process of listing on the stock exchange and the IPO is not an easy process and takes time and resources to follow all the requirement of the local regulator bodies. The listing of the company will also lead to much more requirements for submitting information to the minority shareholders and to the public as a whole. This will increase the operating expenses.

The process however has also it benefits. The company will be forced to become more transparent and it is good for the investors. It reduces their risk. Now on the Bulgarian stock exchange there is an option even smaller companies, even startups to be listed on the stock exchange on a special segment. They can raise up to 1 mill euros and the requirements for the documentation are much simpler. For me listing on the stock exchange is a very good option to raise financing and to attract investors if you plan to be correct with the small investors. Until the Bulgarian company owners don't understand that that concept they will have hard time to raise money for their business on the stock exchange.

Management Buy-out (MBO)

This is comparatively new form for exit of the owner, especially in Eastern Europe. Here we have a situation where the owner of the company wants to exit the business because he is tired or for some other reason. At the same time he had set up a good top management team which wants to continue working and developing the business. The best part is that these people know the business very well and they can make a clear estimation what is the value of the company and its potential. The issue is that even the highest paid managers will have difficulties to come up with the whole amount which is necessary to buy the company they are working for. That's why usually in MBO cases the managers are supported with financing either by a bank or by a private equity fund. This is also the best option for the fund because they will have a management team which is ambitious and which knows the business inside out. In Bulgaria we had several such transactions with the MBO scheme. A chain of radio stations and a dairy company. In both cases the foreign owners exited the firm and sold it to the local management.

Management Buy-In (MBI)

Here we have a similar situation to the one in MBO case but the difference is that the management team is outside for the company. Although they are not part of the current management these managers most probably have experience in the same industry and already have proven that they can manage companies successfully. Again the management team will be supported for the financing by a bank or by an investment fund. In both cases, the MBO and MBI the management team also invest some personal money. So they have some financial stake in the whole operation

Employees

There is an option to sell your company to your employees. This is not easy to happen in Bulgaria and in Europe as a whole. It is more common practice in the USA. Have in mind that in such process the first stage of the transaction will take longer time and it will be for a comparatively small stake in the company. The employees need time in order to pay back the owner from the profits they generate from running the company. I have seen a couple cases where the owner had given 10-20% to his employees but to exit the whole company through selling it to its employees I haven't seen in Bulgaria. But it is a theoretical option and that's why I included it in the list of exit options.

Individual Investors

In the beginning of the chapter we said that we can divide the investors on Institutional and Individual groups. We can define a new group of possible buyers for your business in your home country and these are the wealthy people. These people either have some type of profitable business, have generated some cash, and now are looking for opportunities where to invest the free cash or they had a business which they have sold and now are looking for a new opportunity. In the first case the potential investors are looking for more passive source of income. They don't want to run it on an operating level. For example to buy an office building with tenants or to invest in s renewable energy project. If you have such business don't concentrate just on the institutional buyers (financial or strategic) but also look for wealthy people who has some free cash. In the second case these investors might have been in your situation. They were tired and they sold their business. After they took a break for a couple of years their hands started itching because the mind of the entrepreneur never stops working and they start looking around for a new business which to develop. The so called serial entrepreneurs.

Turnaround/ restructuring

Sometimes your business has financial difficulties and most of the potential investors which we have listed so far wouldn't have an interest in it. It is clear that you company doesn't have much value but it still has some assets and most probably business opportunities. Around the world there are companies or management teams which are dealing with turnaround or restructuring of companies. These teams buy the company for a minimum amount and very often they buy the companies for 1 euro. They restructure the firm, develop it, make it profitable and in several years can sell it to an investment fund or a strategic buyer. I also have similar experience. In 2009-2010 together with managers from Germany we wanted to restructure the biggest Bulgarian plastic pipes producer. First I worked together with the German team but they got into some disagreements with the owner and that's how I became the Interim Manager of the company for four months in 2010. It was not a classical deal because we didn't acquired the company from the owner but we managed to restructure it and to find a buyer who offered the owner a 7 figures amount for the company. Then the owner for some other reasons didn't accept the offer and we got out of the management of the company. After one year the banks got into the company, sold the assets and the firm doesn't exist anymore. So have in mind that there is such option. A turnaround teams to enter and even to buy your business and to restructure it. You as an owner can sell it straight away to such teams or you can hire them as provider of a service. When they restructure the company you will have more options to find a buyer for the company. There are also such funds which specialize in restructuring of companies. So basically any business can be sold. The question is for how much.

EBRD, IFC

The European Bank for Restructuring and Development besides providing financing also can make direct equity investments in companies. It usually makes only minority investments. The bank is not so active in the management of the company and that's why sometimes are preferred by the company owners. Besides their investment horizon is longer than that of the PE and VC funds which also is preferred by the entrepreneurs. It will also be much easier for you as an owner to negotiate to buy back their stake. With the classic PR funds they usually are seeking maximization of their profits and prefer to sell to a third party. In Bulgaria and in almost all Eastern European country EBRD have such investments so it is a viable option.

As you can see there is a variety of potential buyers. Who is the most appropriate for your company depends on your business and mainly on what you want to achieve and on your goals. Don't exclude any group of investors but also don rush to work with all groups because they require different preparation and approach in the negotiations. That's why prepare two list of potential buyers. One which will be with the priority buyers (List A), where you place the investors which you believe will be the best match for you company. If the negotiations don't go well you can also include in the process the potential buyers from your backup list (List B).

How much is the value of my company

Specifics of the company valuation

We reached to the most important moment in the whole process of M&A: The question of how much is the value of your company? I am sure that most probably you as owners are asking yourself very often how much money you can receive for your business. The two questions are related but it is not mandatory that the two values have to be equal. We will get into that moment later in the chapter. In general it will be good if an owner have some basic knowledge and preparation on the topic so that when the buyer comes and ask him how much he wants for the business the company owner doesn't come with some weird number with no argumentation behind it. That's why I dare to say that the company valuation as an issue is mainly for your internal consumption. An owner will know how much most probably he can make if he finds a buyer and this way he will enter the negotiation phase much more prepared. Yes, the valuation report have some impact on the negotiations but at the end the buyer decides how much to pay for your company and he can make his own calculations. I believe that you are aware that in private negotiations there is no way a company valuation, nevertheless how detail it is and who made the valuation, to serve as an official document in the process.

It is a completely different case if you participate in some procedure or auction organized by the government or the municipalities.

In that case the law or some regulations will require an independent valuation of the business or the assets which will be object of the transaction. This is completely different situation form the private talks. A third case is that the bank also wants company valuation when you are asking for a business credit. Very often in the second case and not so often in the bank case some abuses occur. If there is such potential danger the existence of such independent valuation is one of the way the people who might act unethically and even unlawfully to protect themselves for their actions. I assume you are aware that such term as an independent valuation doesn't exist in its pure meaning. It is called independent because it is performed by a third party which is not the seller or the buyer of the asset. If we consider the issue from that point of view then I will agree that the valuation is independent. With all valuation methods which we will discuss in details a little bit there are many subjective factors. For an identical company or asset one appraiser can value the asset for 100 euros, another one for 80 euros and a third one for 120 euro. All of them will do it with no intention for fraud but will have different assumption when they make the valuation. For example different people have various level of tolerance to the risk. Based on that they can use different norms for discounting the cash flows and as a result they will receive different numbers for the value of the firm. It is not against the rules and nobody can accuse the appraiser why he discounted with 15% instead of 18% for example. The most common case is the appraiser to be influenced by the fact who pays for the valuation and what the ordering party has as a goal. As everything else in our life whoever pays for the music chooses the songs. All these stuff are clear to the buyers and that's why even if you have a company valuation done by a world investment bank like Merrill Lynch it still cannot be accepted as a mandatory element. It serves more as an orientation in the negotiations for the price of the company.

It is important to make the distinction that the valuation can be for the whole company or just for separate assets. In most case in Bulgaria are performed valuations for separate assets which has to be sold. I guess the reason is that most deals in Bulgaria are for assets not for whole businesses. Even if the company is not in a bad financial situation the owner can prefer to sell it as assets not as a business. In that case the value of the firm will be higher as assets instead of as a whole business. However, when we have a classic M&A deal the focus is on the whole company/business not the assets and that's why the discussions about valuation in the chapter I will make from that standpoint. It is a paradox that very often family companies have bigger value as separate assets instead of the whole business. The main reason is that the owners don't utilize their assets very effectively. This is an issue all over the world. There is also a specific reason which is related to the lack of regulations or actually not applying the existing regulations for a bankruptcy of a company. In countries like Bulgaria you can sell your assets and just leave the liabilities in the firm and most probably in practice there will be no consequences for the owner. This is the reason why we don't have deals for 1 euro in Bulgaria. From any company a person can make more than 1 euro form its assets (for example sell the two office chairs for 40 euros) and that's why nobody sells his company for 1 euro in countries like Bulgaria.

Who is making the company valuation? It again depends on the specific case. If there is a requirement of the law then there are certified appraisers which make the valuations. This is the case for the government institutions and the public auctions. This practice was introduced in Bulgaria in 1993 when the government had to start the privatization of the state owned companies. Then they needed valuations of the assets/companies which had to be privatized and the valuations had to be done by a third party so there is no conflict of interests. This practice is pretty much the same in all Eastern European countries because of the privatization process. Perhaps since in the beginning the goal was to evaluate assets these licensed appraiser when they do valuation for various public tenders still emphasize more on methods which are used for separate assets than on the cash flow of the business. When there is no requirement by law then the company valuation can be performed by any expert which has experience and knowledge in the M&A field. Pretty much it depends on whom you as an owner will trust to make a valuation of your business. There is no licensing regime or special requirements. Pretty much identical situation to the one with real estate brokers.

Another characteristics of the company valuations is that they are always done for 100% of the company. Even if somebody wants to buy just 60% or 30% of the company the valuation is made for the whole business and based on it the two parties can make additional calculations what will be the value of the stake which is an object of the transaction.

Despite all subjective elements and the fact that it is not pure mathematical process, the company valuations follow some major principles. If one M&A consultant/appraiser doesn't want to ruin his name which is his main assets, he will try to follow these rules and to make really an objective valuation. In general the company valuations depends on the following factors:

The perspectives in front of the business
The perceived risk for the company
The price of the capital or the available alternatives
The risk of the country in which the company operates
The financial results of the company

Here I want to get into more details in the biggest misunderstanding which I see in the company owners in regards to the valuations we make for their companies. Very often as part of the preparation process and the management consulting projects we do for them we discuss with the owners the strategic options which they have in from of their business. As a result hey want to make a valuation of their company and after we are ready with the report and the valuation they tell us: "Great, so the value of the business is 10 mill. But we also have a very strong brand so can you make a valuation also on our brand?" Another point they make is: "Our office building most probably also worth a lot of money". This is a big mistake. As I mentioned in the beginning of the chapter there are two approaches. Either you make a valuations of all assets (fixed and non-fixed) or you make a valuation of the company as a business entity. As you know any business is aggregation of all assets and all liabilities. Thanks to the assets which the company possess it makes some revenues and profits. Here you also include the brand which I mentioned earlier. If Coca-Cola has a strong brand it definitely helps it to make a lot of sales. If Coca-Cola wants we can take it out it as a separate asset and sell it to a third party for very good money. However, without that brand the value of the business of Coca-Cola for sure will not be the same because now the company without the brand will make a lot less sales and profits. Whether to sell the company as a whole business or as separate assets is a decision of the owner but no investor will agree to mix the two things. To value the company based on its cash flows and also to add the value of separate assets.

In regards to that the three main groups of valuation methods are:

Assets based methods. Here you can include the balance value of the assets, the replacement method, the liquidation method, etc

Market method – here the market indicators of the company are compared to the ones of other participants on the market. For example the rations Price/EBITDA or revenues/EBITDA, etc

Income methods – here you make valuation of the

business based on the cash flows which the company make from its activities.

We already discussed that based on the type of deals we make and the fact that we concentrate on good and profitable companies I prefer the methods in the second and in the third group. In our practice we use them for a valuation of the companies we work with. Now I will discuss in more details the main methods which are used when somebody is making a company valuation

Company valuation methods

The correct approach is one valuation never to be based only on one valuation method. That's why every experienced M&A consultant is using several methods and he comes with the final value by putting relative weight of each method. What relative weight to give to each of the methods is a subjective issue and it is left on the personal judgment of each consultant.

DCF model (Discounted cash flow). This is the preferred method by me and I believe by most M&A consultants which are preparing company valuations. Why is that? A person or a fund is buying a certain business mainly because they want to make some money out of it. It doesn't matter what the industry is, what the assets are, where the company is located, etc. Actually it might matters because each investor has his own preferences but the leading factor is the amount of money he would make. Sometimes people buy business with other intention besides profit. For example it is a public secret that most media nowadays cannot sustain themselves as profitable organizations but still many investors want to buy such business because the media is also a tool for having influence in the society. However, in the typical case the investor cares how much money he will make from his investment. We can check how much is the current net profit of the company but it won't be the best indicator for our investment decision. First this is already a past event.

The current profit is a fact and it will most probably be distributed to the current owner through a dividend. Nobody knows for sure if next year the profit will be the same and the buyer is interested what will happen with the company from the moment he buys it forward. Besides the current investor might have invested significant money into new machines and equipment and the benefits of that investment will show up in the financial results in the next 4-5 years. The investment is made now and it affects the current profit negatively but the benefit will be in the future. If you are the current owner you won't find it fair if your company is valued based on the profit from last year, right? The fairest approach will be to forecast what revenues your companies will generate in the next 4-5 years, what profits it will make and these cash flows to be discounted so that they are presented at their present value. We all know that one euro in five years will have much less value than one euro right now. Even if it is just for the inflation. If you are using the DCF method for valuation and you have just signed a big contract with a client for the next three years the profits from this step will be taken into account in the company valuation. Besides the sum of the discounted cash flows of the company for the next five years the appraiser also has to add towards your company value and another component.

This is the residual value of the firm or you can see also as a terminal value. I am not sure if you are familiar with these jargon and I will try to explain it with simple words. Any company is supposed to exist even after the five years for which we have forecasted its revenues and profits. Basically here the consultant applies the principle of ongoing concern and that's why it is normal to add a value which to be added to the sum of the five years of cash flows. When you add the two numbers you will receive the final valuation of the company based on the DCG model. I mentioned several times that the sum of the future cash flows and also the terminal value has to be discounted. The question is with what percentage to discount them? This is a very subjective issue and a consultant can play with various assumptions. As a result he can "manipulate" the company valuation. In general the discount rate has two components. A risk-free component and an equity premium. For the risk free components as a benchmark the consultants usually use the interest rates of the government bonds. For the equity premium is a little bit more complex and it mainly depends how risk –averse is the investor and what yield he is expecting for his investment. We talked in the previous chapter that the financial investors like the PE funds are expecting an annual yield of 15-20% and that's why they use these numbers as discount rate for their valuations.

There are two more issue which we have to pay attention to because they have a significant impact on the DCF model. They also contribute to the fact that the DCF model is the most objective method for a company valuation. When you buy a business it is also important to calculate what investments (CAPEX) you must make in order to keep the current level of profitability of the company. Let's take for an example you have bought a company for 10 mill euros and it is making 1 mill euros net profit. So basically you have calculated that within 10 years you will be able to return the invested money and that suits you perfectly. That's OK but perhaps in 2 years you must buy new machines for 3 mill euros. If you don't do it the company most probably won't be able to keep making 1 mill euros net profit per year. So actually the money which you have to invest in acquiring that business will not be 10 mill but 13 mill euros and your yield will not be 10% but more of 7%. The same principle also applies for the working capital. If the financial reports reveals that now the company is having 5 mill euros turnover but it is planning to have 8 mill turnover in three years most probably the new owner has to "close" more money in working capital in the firm. The DCF model is taking these specifics into account and the final valuation you will receive through that method is the most objective one.

EBITDA multiple (Earnings before interest, taxes, depreciation, and amortization). This is one of the key abbreviations which you will come across in the process of mergers and acquisitions. This is actually a very easy and fast method to calculate the rough valuation of your company and that's why it is very popular as a tool. It is very likely that you will hear from a friend or from the press that somebody has sold his company for five times EBITDA. This method also shows how much money you are making from your business but unlike the DCF model the EBITDA is directed to the past results of the company. Basically you can analyze how profitable was your company in the past years but if this will continue in the future the EBITDA cannot reveal. Another disadvantage of the EBITDA is that it doesn't take into account the capital expenditures in the changes in the working capital which can be a significant item in the future. When you are using the DCF model you have to fill a table with some data and also to make some calculations. With the EBITDA method you just have to multiply two numbers and you can come up with the company valuation. The question is with how much to multiple the EBITDA of the company.

Well there is no clear answer. You can find out what is the normal multiple for the various industry and companies but again it will be an average of many deals. Since a huge amount of the deals are done by financial investors and they are looking or 15-20% yield very often the deals multiple are in the 5-7 times range. Of course there deals which take place at ten times EBITDA but also you can buy a company at 3-4 times. There are some factors which have to be taken into consideration when you calculate the multiple but at the end everything ends up in private negotiations between the two parties. There are two main rules which you can use as guidance when you negotiate the multiplier for your company. If the EBITDA margin of your company is high than you can expect a higher multiple. This depends mainly from the industry you operate in but also from the management of the company. For example a software company is normal to have 3-4 mill euro EBITDA when it has 10 mill euros sales. So it will have 30-40% EBITDA margin. At the same time a salami producer who also has 10 mill euros in sales is normal to have an EBITDA of only 1 mill euro. The bigger the EBITDA margin is it means that if you increase your sales with one million then your net profit will increase with a much bigger number. This is the key indicator. How much profit you make not how much turnover you have. That's why if the company has higher EBITDA margin the investor is more inclined to give you a higher multiple for the EBITDA.

The other rule is to see what is the growth of the EBITDA as an absolute amount in the last 3-4 years. If the EBITDA is growing as an absolute amount the investor will again be inclined to give you a bigger multiple. He knows that even if he buys the company now with 1 mill euros EBITDA then most probably it will have 2 mill euros EBITDA in five years. Sometimes company owners which companies neither have high EBITDA margin nor their EBITDA is growing tell me that they want to sell their company at 10 times EBITDA. I am explaining them that if an investor pays 10 times EBITDA it means that he should be OK with 10% annual yield. For such level of yield they have more secure alternatives such as investing in real estate projects. That's why if the investors are buying a company which doesn't grow they will expect higher profitability compared to the other less risky alternatives This means they will expect smaller multiple of EBITDA for your company.

Multiplier of the sales – for some businesses it is more appropriate to use multiple of sales instead of EBITDA. For example your business to be sold for 1.5 times net sales or 0.7 times net sales. In a little bit I will give you some examples.

Methods of comparable – Here the idea is that if a company which is very similar to yours has been sold for 5 mill euros then your company value also should be 5 mill euros. As you know the most objective criteria for valuation of an item or a company is what the market says about it. I assume that the first thing which you say when you are trying to sell you apartment is that the neighboring apartment was sold for 200 000 euros and this way you imply that your apartment also should be sold for the same amount. The problem is that it is hard to compare even two apartments and when we are comparing two companies is becoming much more complex. In the comparison model factors like the management, where the company is located, and its perspective for development have huge impact on the valuation of a business.

Even some items which are invisible for the people who didn't participate in the deal matters. If you are operating in small country like Bulgaria there might not be many public information about done deals. Then you have to use data and examples from bigger markets like USA. It won't be appropriate to say that Nestle was sold for example 10 times EBITDA and that's why your confectionery business also has to be sold for 10 times EBITDA. The potential risk for your business from the fact that it is much smaller than Nestle and that it is located in a country like Bulgaria is much bigger than the risk of investing in Nestle. Although it is not perfect the comparison method is an easy and quick way to get an initial orientation for the expected price of your company. Here the experts use some variations like price to net profit or price to balance value of your assets. In the end the idea is to compare your business with similar companies.

Book value of your assets. With this method we already switched to the methods which emphasize not so much on the business side of the company but more on the assets. Each company as you know has assets and liabilities and for each item in the balance sheet there is a specific number. The idea of this method is that if we decide tomorrow to sell off all our assets and to pay all our liabilities there should be something left for us as owners. Expert call that value the net worth of the company which is the sum of the capital of the firm plus the reserves it accumulated from profits or revaluations of assets. This amount should be for you after the transaction. Of course in the balance sheet you have assets which are fully depreciated and have zero value for tax purposes but they still can be sold for some money. That's why there is a sub method which is actually calculating the adjusted book value of the assets according to the market value.

Liquidation value. This calculation is somewhat similar to the book value except it value assumes a forced or an orderly liquidation of assets instead of book value. The overall value of the business that uses that method should be lower than the value calculated by the book value. The reason is that when a business is liquidated you can be forced to act fast and to accept offers which might be not so favorable. Even if an asset has a balance value of 100 euros it might take you months until you find a buyer and very often you don't have so much time and accept the first offer.

Method of replacement. Very often for you as an owner it is not so important what is the book value or the liquidation value of a certain assets but for how much money you have to pay to replace it. Besides the price of the machine you might have expenses related with its launching in exploitation or potential losses from the time during which you had to replace the equipment. That's why for any business owner is important to know actually what it will cost him to replace one asset with another one.

As I mentioned usually the M&A consultant uses a combination of several methods and is preparing a written document. In this report you have the following main parts:

Title page
Summary of the valuation
Analysis of the economic outlook
Industry analysis
The used assumptions for the various factors for the valuation
The used methods of valuation
Weighting the results from the various methods and what is the final number for the valuation of the company
Not all of you have big companies and perhaps for some of you it won't be justifiable to prepare a separate valuation

report. In regards to that there are some rules which you can use as guidelines and which can show you how much the value of your business would be. Have in mind that since we are talking for smaller business the risk for their bankruptcy will be bigger and as a result the valuation which you will receive will be lower than what your friends have told you or what you have read in the press for the big deals. The way how the owner of a confectionery business with 30 mill turnover cannot compare himself with Nestle the same way if your company has sales of 1 mill cannot compare to another local company which has 30 mil sales. Here are the guiding rules for the various types of business.

Restaurants

Here we have in mind full scale restaurants, the one which have waitresses. It is not easy to give an exact formula because you have such variety of restaurants. It is also not so common to find a restaurant which is profitable and the owner is not participating actively in its management. There are such cases but then we are talking for restaurants which have at least 1-2 mill turnover. Whoever buys a restaurant have to know that he has to be involved with it 7 days per week. You as an owner of a resultant know that fact very well. Perhaps you know what a famous anecdote is saying: "There are two types of bartenders. Those who are stealing and those who are stealing a lot" The key item of the valuation of each restaurant is its location. Another factor which has a significant impact is the rent which you are paying. The general rule of thumb is the rent not to exceed 10% of the turnover of the restaurant. The

condition of the equipment also matters. With all these conditions we can say as rule of thumb that the value of a restaurant should be:
30-35% of the annual turnover plus the goods
2-3 times EBIT
2.5-4 times EBITDA

Medical practices

Here we can also include the dentist practices. This is one of the hardest type of business for sale because it is very dependable on the owner. You have to be careful about the licenses which the business owns and if they are transferable to another owner. I assume it is clear that we are not talking here for big hospitals or individual practices but for small medical centers. In that business besides the owner you also have several other employees. So we have a small business with employees, not a personal practice which in pretty much not transferable at all. Because of the big range in the prices of the services as a result of the quality of the person who provides the service the best rule of thumb is to sell the medical practice for 40-45% of the annual turnover plus the inventory.

Auto repair shops

Here as a rule of thumb you can use that an auto repair shop should be sold for 25-30% of the its turnover plus the inventory or 3-4 times EBITDA. It is important what is the expertise of the technicians and how many of them will stay in the shop if the owner is changed. You might buy such business and in three months the technicians leave and you will have just some fixed assets left, but not much business.

Small hotels, B&B types.

What matters here is whether the business is seasonal or it is all year round. It is also of key importance what the size of the hotel is. It is clear that we are not talking for the big hotels but whether you have 8 rooms or 30 rooms is crucial for the effectiveness of the business and its value respectively. Here the price can be either 4-5 times EBITDA or a certain amount per room. This amount depends on how many stars the hotel has, what its occupancy rate is, etc. From a professional standpoint this is the most objective criteria when you value a small hotel. Therefore I would advise to use a sum per room instead of a multiple of EBITDA as an indicator for valuation.

In general the smaller a business is the harder it is to make the right valuation and it is also harder to transfer it to another owner. That's why in such cases I am more OK with the practice to value these business as a sum of some assets instead of cash flows or as ongoing businesses. If you insist on valuing a small business as a big company you might end up in the situation that 6 months after the deal a significant part of the business to be gone. The clients just followed the old owner and you are left only with assets.

When you are preparing a valuation of you company you have to be aware that whatever amount the valuation reports states the potential buyer will want to negotiate with you the price. Even if your valuation is conservative the expectations of the buyer will be that you have exaggerated a little bit and that's why he should negotiate a discount. From a psychological point of view any person wants to feel well that he managed to get some bargain deal. That's why it is normal practice your valuation to be one idea higher than what you really would like to receive for your business. Now the valuation report which your M&A consultant prepared despite all this conditionality might be lower than your expectations. At the end the consultant has to try to be fair and objective in order to act as a professional.

His job should not be to please you. Here we are not having the case where he can increase the valuation a little bit so that you have room for negotiations. If the gap between the valuation and your expectations is very big than you as an owner have to think if it will make sense to start the M&A process at all. Because of that possible outcome the valuation is usually done before the launch of the process together with the teaser and the information memorandum. If the valuation doesn't suits you either you have to accept the facts or to make some changes so that you improve the financial results of your company, which will increase its value. If your M&A consultant is a professional he will not create a valuation which will please you but he will make an objective one. If the valuation is not objective he knows that the chance to sell your business will be minimal and most probably after all efforts which you and he has to put in the process there will be no closed deal. Whatever offer you receive it will not meet your expectations as an owner. A professional consultant wants to close any deal because the success fee is the moment where he makes his real money not the small retainers he will charge you for the teaser, the IM and the valuation report. Consultant goal is not to pump up your ego with high valuation but to make money.

An important factor in preparing the valuation report is the condition of your financial statements. At the end all income methods step on your official financial statements. If what a consultant or an investor can see in the official statements doesn't comply on 100% with the real numbers of the business (for whatever reasons) then it will be hard to defend that the valuation of your business is fair. There are also tools which can help to solve this problem but it is a risk for the buyer and it shows unprofessional management of your company which will result into a price discount.

Since we are talking all the time for the value of your company it is very important to say that there is sometimes a huge difference between the value of your company and how much you will receive as an owner. Somehow, by default the company owners believe that if we tell them that the company valuation is 10 mill euros and they will receive 10 mill into their personal bank accounts when the deal closes. Actually the money they will receive are calculated with the help of the following formula

My money = Company valuation – financial debt + cash

Pretty much if you start from the company value then you have to add all the cash which the company has into its bank accounts and to take out the amount of all bank credits and financial leasing (financial debt in general). This way you will receive the amount which the new owner can transfer to your personal bank account. A lot of companies might be valued at 50 million euros but the owners to receive only 10 or 20 million euros for them. To make it clearer let's take the following example. You have a 3 bedroom apartment in a nice neighborhood which is valued 500 000 euros. If it is furnished it is normal to receive a slightly better price for it. This is actually the cash which the company has in the bank accounts. At the same time you have a mortgage for the apartment in the amount of 300 000 euros. Here you will have two options.

Either you can pay in full the mortgage to the bank and the new owner will receive the apartment free of any financial liabilities or you can agree with the buyer that he will take over the mortgage but then he will pay you only 200 000 euros for the apartment. In both cases the final amount for you will be the same and which option to choose will depend on other factors. There is no way that you will receive 500 000 euros cash for your apartment although it is its market value. That's why it is important to make a difference between the value of the company or the money which the owner will receive for his business. The latter amount is also called equity value of the business. If you are selling only a stake from the company after you have agreed on the value of the whole company it is easy to calculate what will be the amount for the stake which the buyer wants to acquire. This doesn't mean that all calculations have to be proportional. For example it is normal practice to have a premium if you are selling a majority stake in the firm.

In summary, the company valuation is important component but it is not the only factor for the successful closure of an M&A transaction. It is more important for the financial investors. When you are negotiating with a strategic buyer you can also emphasize not only on the financial numbers but also on the synergies which your business would have if it became part of their big structure. If you manage to do it and convince them in the synergy effect most probably the price they will pay for your company will look unrealistically high if you calculated based on the discussed valuation methods in the chapter. Any outside observer will wonder why the investor paid so much for that company and he will surprised that the company was sold for 10 or 15 times EBITDA. They reason is that the only info he will see is just the financial numbers That synergy cannot be seen from the valuation report and it is hard to measure it because it varies from one potential investor to another potential investor.

Negotiations and structuring of the deal

This is the stage where it is the hardest to set up some rules and guidance because you have such variety of companies and situations. Иt is impossible to say how a deal will proceed and how much time it will take. You can say that this is the stage where you and your consultant has to apply more art than science. However there are several key moments and I will get into more details for each of them. These moments are: finding an investor and getting their interest, a visit and a meeting with the potential investor, negotiations, and submission of the initial offer. All these stages can take from 1-2 months to 6-12 months and we are talking just for negotiations stage of the whole M&A process. That's why you don't have to be surprised that we didn't have a case where we closed a deal for less than 6 months.

The question here is whether we should use firm deadlines for each of these sub stages or to be more flexible. When you are reading about the big deals in the press you find out that by a certain date the interested parties are required to submit an offer. For each sub stage there are firm deadline which the potential buyers have to follow. In the previous chapters I mentioned that it is good idea to have some approximate timeframe for each stage of the process so that you can have it under control. However for the smaller deals, for family owned businesses, I would not recommend to have firm deadline as it is the case with the big investment banks. Actually the whole concept for organizing an auction and have distinct stages in the process is applicable only when your company has clear advantages and generate significant interest. The whole book which describes the steps of an M&A process is based on that assumption. The truth is that for most companies there is no line of interested buyers and very often the owner is forced to talk to just one potential buyer. If you fall in this situation it is impossible to create an auction with some deadlines for the various sub stages.

Finding potential buyers

You have already prepared the necessary documents and your consultant has prepared the two lists with potential buyers. Now is the time to attract their intention and to get them interested in your investment opportunity. Although for the smaller deals, under 5 mill euros, it is hard to have a structured process with fixed deadline it is still a good idea informally to try to imitate such process. What do I mean? When the interested investors ask you if there are some deadline when they have to submit their offer or to do a due diligence you don't tell them that you have one. However, you try to lead the process in such way that all participants are pretty much at the same stage in the M&A process. Some of the investors will be very fast in their actions because that's what they do for living and their teams are comparatively small. For example the private equity and the VC funds. That's what they do as a business. In general the strategic investors are slower in the process because their decision has to be coordinated with many departments. Another point is that the investors which are located in your home country can be much faster than the ones which are from abroad. Some of the buyers will have much bigger interest and motivation in the possible acquisition and that's why they will act faster. In order to be able to perform your strategy of informal action you must take into consideration all these points so that you can receive several offers pretty much at the same time.

This will be the perfect case for you and will be put in the strong position in the M&A process. If you don't organize an action you can have a potential buyer who is very interested and submits his offer early in the process. This offer might be the best one which you will receive from all interested parties but the human nature of a person will make him to act greedy. You would like to see if somebody of the other potential buyers won't submit a better offer and wait for it. While you are trying to receive offer from the other buyers the first investor might get nervous and to pull out his offer and leave the process. The buyers don't like to be put in a situation where they have to compete between themselves.

How to get in touch with the buyers? You are not selling an apartment to put an ad in the newspaper. The process is confidential and that's why you must have individual talks with each interested investor. Some of them you or your consultant will know personally. Others will be unknown guys. In both cases the contact is personal and it will require the signing of a confidentiality agreement. I wouldn't recommend to use any web site or platform for a company sale unless your company is really small and the deal can be considered more of a "commodity" deal. Let's say you have a restaurant and there are tens or hundreds similar restaurants in your city. In this case it is OK to announce the sale on a specialized platform. Having in mind the psychology and the perception of most people that a company is sold when it has financial troubles such listing on a platform might have a negative effect on your operating activities and on your current clients.

Now I can recall a case for a Bulgarian mineral water bottling company. There was an information in the media that the company is for sale. A reporter called the owner and she denied that the company is for sale. Then the reporter called the industry association and the chairman of it said that he is not aware the company to have financial difficulties and that's why doesn't think that the owner decided to sell it. I completely don't understand that perception for when a company to be sold but this is not the important thing now. The interesting part is how the reporter found out about the process. I assume that the owners decided to check and see if there will be any interest in possible acquisition of their company. They have hired somebody who is not a professional M&A consultant to handle this project. For example a lawyer or a real estate broker. I told you that in the M&A process, since the transactions are big in terms of absolute amounts, a lot of people are tempted to act as an M&A advisors. So the owners hired somebody unexperienced with the process and since they didn't have the network decided to put an ad on the platform for sale of businesses of Financial Times. It was an anonymous ad but on one of the pictures a person could see the flag of Bulgaria and the company flag. While the reporter was going though the various listing saw the project and figured out the identity of the company. That's how the whole story started. Because of such cases I would recommend only private contacts and individual talks with each potential investor. No listing on web sites and platforms.

When you make the first contact with the potential investor a significant role will have the M&A consultant which you have engaged for the process. Once he already had created the two lists of potential buyers he could create a simple excel table where both of you can follow at what stage is the relationship with each potential buyer from the two lists. You can add each investor you are already in contact. Which ones have signed NDA and have received the Info memo? Which investors have rejected the opportunity? Do you have difficulties to receive an answer from some of the companies and are you trying to reach the right person in the company? If you write down all this steps in a file, excel or just a word table, it will be much easier for you have an overview of the process. This approach will allow you to achieve the unofficial auction which we talked about earlier.

The visit of your company and a meeting with you.

Some of the investors after they had signed the NDA and had received the information memorandum might have additional questions. You will have to prepare additional reports. I always recommend to meet with the potential buyer as early as possible in the process. Don't hide any information and offer them to come and meet you in person. There is nothing which can substitute the personal contact and I really don't understand how some people expect to make or receive an offer for their business even without a meeting with the current owners of the business. It might work for the big deals but for the majority family owned businesses it hides a lot of risks. Actually when you have a personal meetings both parties are making something like a due diligence on each other. Not only the buyer collects information and feedback about your business but you also are gathering some impressions for the investor. In the beginning of the book we talked that in some cases it might be very important for you who exactly you will sell your company to. Then not only the price will be a factor. That's why I always suggest the owners instead of sending report after report to the potential buyers to offer a personal meeting. At this meeting you can answer all additional questions of the interested investors. Once you agree on the date and time of the meeting it will be helpful to ask the investor to send you in advance the questions and the topics he would like to research further. This way you will be prepared and the meeting will be much more productive. In most cases the investors are doing it by themselves without waiting for you to make such request.

During the visit besides the pure facts and data which you will give to the investors it is also important to leave a good sense of hospitability in the guests. Most of Southern European countries are very hospitable and it is in our nature to try to make them feel very well during the business visit. You can help with the reservations for the hotel, with the travel to your factory, invite them for a lunch or dinner, etc. I am not saying that you have to pay for their hotel but it will be good to make them feel pampered. Most probably in the first visit you will not meet with the owner of the big international company but with some of the managers. After the trip these managers will have to report to the owner or to the board of directors. How and what they will report to them also depends on the fact how they feel after the business trip. The decisions are taken by people not by computers on the base on pure facts and financial data. In general in Bulgaria as a southern country we have no problem with the task to make our quests feel well. In the Anglo-saxonian countries it is a little bit different.

The way how the visit of your factory or whatever business you have passes depends to a big extend whether the visitor is a financial investor or a strategic buyer. If the buyer is a financial player most probably he won't have much idea of the nature of your business and that's why most questions he has will be for your competitors, the industry, the trends, the business plan, your expectation for the next 2-3 years, etc. Questions which will help him to get an idea where he ended up. With the strategic players the visits and the negotiation flow is completely different. These buyers know very well your industry and business and they just need to spend one hour with you in the factory or in the store and they will have a very good idea what should be the value of your company and what can be the synergies with their business. Many times I have been a witness how when I bring a strategic buyer to our client they start making a tour around the factory and talk for hours on their language. My task is just to get out of their way. After the meeting the company owner tells me: "Hey, finally you brought me people who know what I am talking about. Very nice people". With the same company owner a month ago we had a meeting with an investment fund which was interested to buy a stake in the firm. Those financial manager got the owner crazy (his words) with some stupid questions and after the meeting the owner got the impression that these financial gurus didn't know how to turn on the machines in the factory but they are planning to buy his factory.

This is a normal reaction and one of the reason is that a significant part of the family companies are managed by entrepreneurs who don't understand the concept behind the investments funds. The owners believe that all people which are interested to buy their business should be experts in the same filed. Otherwise how they will manage the business. Pretty much the owners don't understand that for the investment fund managers this is all about numbers and calculations. If the numbers make sense they will make the deal without thinking so much what exactly is the nature of the business. They have 10 more companies in their portfolio and the only thing which matters is to make a good return for the insurance and the pension funds which gave them money for management. If the return come from your company or from another company in their portfolio it doesn't matter.

It will be also good if you, as the owner, are prepared for the questions which the potential investors might ask you during the visit. The most common questions are:

Why are you selling? We talked that you must have a very well structure story about this question.

Where is the hidden value in your company? The investor will not ask it so directly but he will try to find the answer on that question.

How long have you been in this business?

What challenges you have in front of your company?

They will ask for some legal, environmental or regulatory problems which you might have and for any expected changes in these fields.

What are your plans for the future?

It is important during these talks and even before the visit when you have submitted information in the IM not to include some confidential information. Eventually nobody knows if these investors have real interest to buy your company or they are just trying to do some market research and a study of their competitors. That's why when they ask for example which are your biggest clients don't tell them any names. You can give them a table with the distribution of the sales among the top clients but instead of names you can wrote: Company A, company B, company C, etc. You are not obliged to provide any information which you believe can hurt your business and there is no problem to tell them directly why you cannot provide it at this stage of the process.

You can provide it at later stage when you are sure that they are not "fishing" and are really interested to buy your business. Of course what type of information to reveal depends also on the type of the interested buyer. You can provide more information to the financial investors. First of all they need it more because they don't know your business and secondly they cannot use it because they are not operating in the same sector and don't compete with you. For the strategic buyers always have something in mind. Besides they should be able to answer themselves most of these questions.

This visit is also an opportunity for you to get to know the potential buyers and that's why you can ask them some of the following questions:

Have you ever bought other similar business?
What happened with these businesses and their development after you have acquired them?
When do they expect or would like to close the deal?
Who is taking the decision on their side for such acquisitions? The owner. The board of the directors or the CEO?
Do they have enough financing and what will be the source of financing for the deal? Are they planning to use bank loans?
What are their plans for your company?

Sometimes you might need to have 2-3 meetings with the potential buyer. First of all if the investor becomes serious then most probably also other people, more senior managers, would have to come and visit your business so that they get to know you. Secondly the process of negotiations will start in full scope and you might need several meetings in order to reconcile your differences. Submitting offers.

After the visit the next step in the process is to negotiate a structure of the deal so that whoever from the investors is interested to be able to submit an offer. The most normal step is in the beginning of the process the potential buyer to ask you how much you want for your company. I am advising our clients not to answer the question directly because at the moment they say a specific number it becomes an anchor. From there on all negotiations more or less will be around that number. It might turns out that that the number is smaller than what you could receive as an offer. On the other side it can be so high that it will scare away the buyers and they give up from submitting an offer. This will be the worst case for you because the price also depends a lot on the way how the deal is structured and some other factors which we didn't discuss yet. Here comes as a handy tool the company valuation which you have prepared in advance. You can give it to the interested buyers and tell them that your consultant has done some calculations on the base of several methods but you believe that despite whatever is written in the valuation report each interested buyer should submit an indicative offer. Each buyer with the bid can also state what his assumptions are and why he is giving you such an offer. This way you can leave the door open for future negotiations.

The offered price sometimes can look very low to you because the interested buyer had understood some information wrong and have calculated some risks which actually don't exist on practice. You can also remind them that now they are submitting only an indicative non-binding bid. Even if you receive a binding bid it will be with a lot of conditions based on the fact that the investor has not performed yet a due diligence for which we will talk in the next chapter. This fact in practice makes each submitted offer non-binding. You goal at this stage has to be to receive as many offers as it is possible. You understand that even if you receive unacceptable offer form a certain buyer the process with him doesn't end. You goal must be to have many opportunities from which to choose from. What should you do if there is a big difference in the submitted offers and your expectations? There are several tools which you can use in order to converge the two positions. Very often the company owners are having some expectation for a certain price because they have a lot of assets in the balance sheet of the company. These assets for real have a significant value but the question is how much they add to the revenues and the profits of the company. Let's take for an example two cosmetics companies. One of them is producing the products in New York City and the other is producing in Ohio. The land, the office building and the production hall in New York cost a lot more than the same assets which are located in Ohio. However, the COGS of the product, its sales, and the profits doesn't differ much of the fact if the toothpaste is produced in Ohio or in New York.

These facts are of no interest to the end client and are not a factor when he chooses which toothpaste to buy in the pharmacy. If you are in such situation and the related office building or manufacturing hall has a very high value because of the location my advice for you will be to take these assets out of the balance sheet and to put them in a separate companies. Then your main company will rent them from the other companies. This way this expensive asset will not be included in the initial deal and you won't consider the proposed offer as too low for the assets which you have. You as an owner can either sell this fixed asset to another investor who is interested in real estate or just you will have another business (real estate business) from which you can receive an annual fixed income. Here you don't have to forget that after you take out this fixed asset out of the balance sheet your company will have additional expense for the rent of this asset. This way the net profit of the company will not be anymore 1 mill euro but let's say 500 000 euros. As a result the company valuation will be lower based on the formulas which we discussed in the previous chapter. This way you will receive a smaller valuation for your business but you will also have an additional income stream. It is a matter of calculation to see if it matters to make this transaction with the moving some of the fixed assets to a separate company. The biggest factor is how valuable you believe that this building is for you. This method applies to all assets which are in your company balance and are not related to the main activity of the company. These assets should be taken out of the company balance in the preparation phase so you decrease the chance to receive an offer which doesn't meet your price expectations.

Very often the investors will give you a lower offer because they are not sure that your company will be able to keep the same turnover and profit in the next 4-5 years. You have calculated that if the company is making 1 mill profit and the investor pays you 10 mill then for 10 years he will be able to pay back his investment. That's is OK but what will happen if the net profit of your company goes down to 500 000 euros after you leave the business. The transaction will not look so attractive to the investor anymore because the investment horizon will go up to 20 years. There is an option that part of the price for the company to be paid to the owner in the form of earn out. This means that the buyer is ready to give you 10 mill for your business but 7 mill he will pay you right now and the rest 3 mill will be paid in the next 2-3 years. The condition is the company to keep the level of profits which you have forecasted in the DCF model and the business plan which you have prepared. If this happen then any buyer will have no problem and he will be happy to pay the 10 mill euros because the numbers work well for him. Sometimes because there is a delay in the payment and also part of the risk is transferred to you there is an option the whole amount of the deal to be increased to 11 mill euros instead of 10. Basically you will have a premium. The earn out scheme is a very common practice but it can be very cunning for the company owners because it depends on how much the new owner will interfere in the operating activities of the company. We can make an analogy with the case that the owner promise to give you one mill euro bonus if you become a champion as a coach of the team but at the same time he sells your two best players because he received very good offers for them. That's why you have to be very careful how you negotiate your earn out scheme but it is used very often as a tool to converge differences in price.

The third tool which you can use in order to converge the difference between the two parties is the form of payment. It can be with cash but also the buyer can pay with shares from his company. As people say "cash is a king" but sometimes it might be hard for the buyer to come up with so big amount with cash in order to pay the whole price. It is not that they doesn't have enough money or business but to be ready with 5 or 10 mill euros in cash even with the support of the bank is not always an easy step. In that situation the buyer can offer to pay a part of the price with his own shares. If the buyer is a public company then it is even much easier to use that scheme. You as an owner will have a liquidity of your shares and after a certain period you can sell the shares on the stock exchange and to take your cash in full. When the buyer offers to include also equity (shares) in the transaction as a form of payment usually there is a premium in the price of the transaction. For example if the price is 10 mill euros all in cash for your business if half of the price can be paid with shares of the buyer then it is normal the whole value of the transaction to be 11 mill instead of 10 mill euros. Usually you will use the current price of these shares on the stock exchange as a benchmark. The downside of that scheme might be that most probably you won't be able to sell those shares right away but have to wait some time. There will be a lock up period.

When you are talking with a strategic buyer try to research his business very well so that you can find some synergy between the two companies. This way even if from financial point of view a certain price to look as unreasonable because of the synergy the board of the directors still can approve the submission of such "generous offer". They will concentrate on the synergies not on the financial formulas.

After you negotiate a little bit with the buyers the next step is to receive a preliminary offer or you can say also as a letter of intent and even term sheet. In the term sheet are outlined the major parameters of the proposed transaction and usually it includes the following components:

The proposed price and the method of payment. These are the elements which we talked about so far. Will there be an earn-out scheme? Will they use only cash for the payment? etc

What actually is buying the investor? Is he buying the whole company or just some assets of it? What percent from the company is he buying? Will there be an option to acquire mores takes in the next stages. Perhaps they want to acquire 100% of the company but to take place on three stages? What will be the conditions so that the payments are executed, etc.

How long will be the due diligence phase and if the investor will get an exclusivity during that period

What warranties the buyer will want from the seller which will be included in the final contract

Will there be an ESCROW? Will there be a deposit. Under what circumstances the M&A process and the preliminary contract can be cancelled? When and how the deposit will be returned?

Will there be conditional payments?

If you accept the offer of one of the interested buyers then you will move to the next stage. It will be great if you had several offers and you could choose. Of course there is a chance that none of the submitted offers meets your expectations. Then you can ask the interested investors to improve their offers or to come back to your reserve list of potential buyers and see if somebody of them might offer you a better proposal. It is also a normal outcome to cancel the process and to improve some things in your business. After some time when you have learned your lessons you can launch the process again. If you are in a situation which makes you to sell your business urgently then you don't have any choice except to accept one of the offers although it doesn't meet your expectations. At the end this is the fair valuation of the market. If nobody gives you the amount you want most probably you don't "deserve" it at this moment.

If you are negotiating with financial investors like the PE funds there are soma additional elements which you have to discuss with them when you agree on the structure of the deal. In most cases the transaction with the investment fund is only the first step of the whole process. You are selling usually just a stake from your company and the reason is that you want to take over the world and you need a financial partner to achieve your goal. As a result you will work with these guys in the next 4-5 years together. You become business partners. That's why it will not be a good tactic both parties to be very aggressive during the negotiation phase with the idea to get the best deal for them. The PE fund can see that you are pressed to the wall, don't have many options at this stage and as a result you will agree to worse terms in the deal. You can sign the deal but you will be left with the feeling that you are screwed up in the deal. As a result since you will continue to run the company on an operating level you can do it in such way that they have no idea what is going on and you will make it up somehow to yourself for the bad terms which they imposed on you.

Unfortunately we had once such case when a PE fund bought a stake in one company for juices and afterwards the two parties sued each other since they had some disputes. You also don't want to press the fund because most probably there will be enough clauses which will give you additional payments to the deal but the fund has to "release" these clauses. That's' why the whole idea and philosophy here should be that you will work together in the next 4-5 years and none of the two parties should feel screwed up when signs the deal. On the other side this is a business and each party is trying to protect its interest and is chasing its goals. Here is a short description of some of the clauses which most probably will be included if you are negotiating a deal with a private equity fund. These clauses will have an effect of the sale of the whole company in several years which is the normal path for any private equity deal.

Tag along drag along rights. As we talked the PE funds have a certain lifespan which is usually 10 years. Within this time they have to make the investment and to exit the company. You can stay in the company forever with your stake but they cannot do it. These tag along drag along rights allows the fund if you find a buyer for the company they can join you in the process. Basically you cannot get rid of your stake and leave them alone in the company. At the same time if the fund decided that it is time to initiate a sale process and to exit the company then you also have to join them. You might believe that this is not the right time and that you have some investment plans but this doesn't matter. If they launch the process and even if you have a majority stake in the company you are required to join them and to sell together the whole company to a third party.

Right of first refusal. You might be in the situation that you are the majority shareholder in the company and you want to sell your stake to John for 5 mill euros. You already signed the term sheet with John. However, if you have such a clause in the contract with the PE fund then you have to offer this stake for 5 mill first to the fund. If they don't want it then you can sell it to John for 5 mill.

Pro rata rights. This is more typical tool for the younger technological companies which sell a stake to a venture capital fund. Since it is very likely that there will be follow-up rounds of financing this clause allows your partner, the VC fund, to participate in the next rounds without diluting its stake. This way they can keep the 15% stake which they have acquired in the first round for example.

Actually from my experience the biggest stumbling stone in the negotiations with the investment funds has been who will have the majority stake. The company owners always want to have at least 51% so that they can call the shots. This desire very often causes heated discussions and at the end the fund managers might tell you: "OK you will have 51% in the company but here is a list of the decisions which has to be taken together". Then they will send a long list of decisions which according to the new article of incorporation has to be taken by the two parties together. This way you think that you are running the show since you have 51% of the capital but in practice you cannot even go to the toilet without the agreement of the investment fund. Here is why several times throughout the book I mentioned that not only the price is the key factor when you negotiate an M&A deal. It is a complex deal and sometimes even a lower valuation can be better for you if you negotiate the other elements in your favor.

Last advices

Here are some last issues which you should pay attention to when you are structuring your deal with the investor:

Don't forget that the main goal is to close the deal. Sometimes the negotiations can get out of control and you can jeopardize the whole process just because somebody is so fixed on a minor issue and he perceive it as a matter of honor for him. It is not important who showed more muscles if the deal fails and both parties risk months of invested resources to go in vain.

Negotiate with the person who takes the decisions. You are the owner of the company and whatever you decide that will happen. Sometimes with the financial investors and very often with the strategic buyers you won't have a direct contact with the people which will take the final decisions about a deal. Try to include them in the process at least on an e-mail level. Otherwise you can end in a situation with the broken telephone. How a person convey the information and explains your position will have a huge effect on the decision which the decision maker will take. Imagine that you want to take a credit from the bank. The decisions are taken on a credit committee meetings. At such meeting it is normal practice to go through 10 cases for a day and those people have never seen you or have visited your company. They have to rely just on the documents and what your credit inspector tells them. The way he present your case will most probably determine if they will give you the credit or not. It is a similar situation with the M&A deals and the decision which the board of directors has to take at a strategic investor.

Negotiations in general are more of an art than science but very often they are the key for the successful closing of a deal or a project. There are various tactics and some people feel more confident in the process. Either because it comes inside them or just because they have a lot of experience in negotiating various deals. The main tool which actually puts you in a stronger or in a weaker position in the negotiations is your BATNA (best alternative to negotiate a deal). While you are negotiating with somebody you still can work on your alternative solutions because it gives you more opportunities. It is even like playing cards. You might be very bad at poker but if you have only strong cards it will be hard for anybody to beat you.

Sometimes you can use your M&A consultant as a cover or as an excuse. It is a dangerous tactic and you have to be in full synchrony with him. It is like playing the game of the good cop and the bad cop. You consultant is in charge of the negotiations and he is taking the battles under your strict orders. But he is the dog which barks. At one point if the process reach a dead point you can call the decision maker of the buyer side and to tell him: " Let's get rid of these consultants and lawyers and let's sit down and we can reach an agreement between us. These consultants advised me what to do but I actually didn't want things to be done exactly that way". That's why you can get out of the dead end situation and not to lose face as the Chinese say. However if you don't agree on this with your consultant in the beginning this tactic can backfire because your team will feel betrayed.

Don't forget that any M&A process is a long and it is like a roller coaster. One day it looks like that everything will fail that there will be no deal and on the next day you receive a written letter from another interested strong potential investor. So, be prepared for such moments of low and high moods.

Choose your battles and if it is necessary compromise. As we discussed you might agree on a lower valuation but not to agree to sign some of the rights we discussed for the PE funds.

Be careful how often you bluff during the negotiations because this is not a poker and at some point you can be caught. You might have sold just a stake and then you are still in the game. Even if you sold the whole company it is very likely that you will have an earn-out scheme and some warranties in the contract. Therefore be careful what you are bluffing about because you might not receive your follow-up payments. If you are selling just assets then the risk is smaller.

When you conduct the negotiations you have to be careful not only for your words but also for the nonverbal communication. According to the psychologists around 80-90% of the communication between the people is not verbal so observe very closely your opponents in the negotiations. That's why I am a big fan on the persona meeting not on taking decision just based on papers.

There is a whole new sector in the M&A process which is actually the first word of the acronym M&A– mergers. Now when I am thinking about it very few deals might be really called mergers and I can't hardly remember any deal in Bulgaria. Yes, in the world you have such deals which are considered mergers, not acquisitions like the deal Daimler-Chrysler but it is still questionable. Since the idea of the book is to be practical and to prepare you for potential deal not to make you an expert in the process of mergers and acquisitions I will not discuss the mergers deals. If you end up in such situation this means that your business is really big and complex and most probably you cannot do it by yourself. People who will guide you down this road will know how to execute a merger and will help you with that.

The preparation of the company, your company financial results, and your skills in negotiations are all factors which will have an impact on the results of the negotiations of the best deal for you. There is no doubt about it. However, the biggest factor which the investors are feeling and it is called FOMO (fear of missing out). In other words the feeling that they will miss on a good deal. This applies in full extend to the financial investors but also sometimes for the strategic investors. Recently we had a project and we were trying to convince a strategic investor to make an offer. It found all the time some excuses not to submit an offer.

At one point one of their competitors made a meeting with our client and they were preparing their offer. Right away the strategic investor which we were waiting for two months to submit an offer gave me a call and told me: "hey we also want to submit an official offer". How did they find out about the second investor I have no idea. Bulgaria is a small country and people are talking. Therefore the value of your company depends mainly on two factors. The first one is the financial results of the company and the second one is how many interested potential buyers you have lined up in the process. So try to use the FOMO factor.

Due Diligence

What is due diligence?

You have found a buyer with whom you have agreed on the deal terms and now you are ready to celebrate. You have to wait a little bit longer though, especially if you are selling a business not assets. During the last month you have provided information to the buyer in terms of standard documents as information memorandum or have answered questions. During all this time the buyer has taken for granted all the information you have given to him and he didn't doubt any facts or data which was released from your side. However, before the buyer pays you the money they would like to double check on the information you have provided and make sure that you didn't lie to them or at least didn't mislead them. That's why they will conduct due diligence on your company. It is not mandatory that you have misled them on purpose. Sometimes this happens because of ignorance on some key issues. For example you don't know how to calculate correctly EBITDA and this is a key indicator for the value of the business. That's why the chosen buyer is provided usually with a couple of month to check the correctness of the provided info. During that period he send his team to check your documents. Very often the period of due diligence has to be extended beyond the two month period but we will discuss why it happens like that with the family businesses. Usually the buyer is hiring a local team because they are familiar with the local regulations and the team is comprised of auditors, lawyers, tax experts and sometimes industry experts. If the buyer is a strategic player they can also send some people from their HQ which are familiar with the business.

The team can be comprised form people from different companies or very often when the deal is big the buyer can hire one of the big four auditing companies which can provide a complete service for due diligence. In most cases the buyer is the side which is paying for the due diligence and very often it is not a cheap exercise. The price is usually in the range of 20-50 000 euros. That's why it is normal practice before the chosen buyer to decide to make that investment to request to receive exclusivity so that you don't talk to other potential investors while he is performing due diligence. In order to receive an exclusivity it will be good if he has made a binding offer and even better of he put some deposit for the deal. If these two condition are not available the company owner might not feel so comfortable to give the buyer an exclusivity. It is true that the cost is taken by the buyer but still the company owner has to tell all other interested investors that he cannot talk anymore with them and kind of turn them down. In general he will limit his opportunities for the future. There is no guarantee that they will be still interested to continue in the process in 3-4 months. Because of that sometimes the process of due diligence is moved forward and is performed by several potential investor.

This happen before they submit the binding offers. If you as an owner choose that approach than the process will become more complex and most probably you will have to rent a virtual data room? What is that room? In general you will have two options how to conduct the diligence nevertheless if it is with one chosen buyer or with several potential investors. In the first option the chosen buyer together with his team will come to your physical premises and will check the documents of the company. If it is only one investor this could be OK but imagine if three teams come to your premises and try to perform due diligence. What will happen? First it is very likely that your employees will find out that you are trying to sell the company and the deal is still not closed. So it is not a sure thing. Therefore it is still better to keep everything in a confidential mode. Secondly the three teams will bump into each other during the process. They can exchange some information between themselves to see where everybody is standing in the process and in terms of deal terms. Plus it will be hard to organize the process in such way that each team has access to the documents without being an obstacle for the other two teams. If you organize a virtual data room then the whole company documentation is scanned and it is uploaded in the cloud. This way the investors from their offices will have access to all documents at any time and can go through each document they need. Besides that software allows much bigger confidentiality and traceability of all actions. You can put different level of access of the various documents so not the whole team will have access to all papers.

Besides you will also know when and who has read a specific document. All these things makes the whole process much easier and save time for you and mostly for the buyers. This is the reason why even in new markets like in Eastern Europe this practice of using virtual data room is getting popularity not only for the biggest deals. The price of that service varies and there are some expensive providers. However, you can also find some platforms, mainly from Indian guys, which provide the basic functionalities of a data room at a very reasonable price. I would strongly recommend you to use virtual data room if the deal you will negotiate is more complex and especially if you expect to have offers from several buyers. If you are selling assets or your business is small you can get away without virtual data room. Yes, most probably the lawyers of the buyer will have to check the ownership documents of the assets for sale but it will be something very quick and most probably you don't have to give exclusivity and you can omit the whole stage with the due diligence in the M&A process.

The due diligence as a stage is much more important for the financial investors because they are not familiar with your business and there is much bigger risk for them that they can encounter some skeletons in the wardrobe. It will not be easy for them to decide whether what they have seen from their visits and what you have told them in the talks matches as information. As a result the due diligence phase with a financial investors takes longer time and it is much more thorough. The strategic investors know your business and they know what they can expect and will find out very easy if you have pulled their leg during the negotiation stage. The managers of the strategic buyers use the due diligence phase as an insurance tool. It doesn't matter how well they know the target companies. Perhaps they have worked together as trade partners for 10 years. There is always a chance that something unexpected will show up later after the closure of the deal. If this happen then the board of the directors will accuse the managers that they intentionally didn't perform due diligence on your company because they wanted to hide something. That's why in order to be safe the managers of the strategic investors also conduct due diligence. Besides they also can come across an interesting info which they overlooked in the previous stages.

It is important to point out that during the due diligence phase, nevertheless if it is done online or on premises, the potential buyers don't have access to your employees and cannot talk to them without your consent. The process is not closed yet so it will be better as few people as possible know about it.

As a seller you also have some expenses in the due diligence stage. If you decide to use a virtual data room then the seller is the side which will have to secure the tool. Besides your team also has to participate in providing the documents and the information and this takes time which is an expensive resource. Sometimes the seller decides to conduct an initial due diligence for himself as part of the preparation stage. This will allow him to identify some potential problems and to take care of them in advance. This way in the real due diligence he will be more prepared and will expect less discrepancies. The preliminary due diligence will decrease the risk of failure of the negotiated deal. You are already aware that this due diligence stage is an expensive exercise for both parties and it works sometimes as an additional motivation for both sides to close the deal successfully. Sometimes the buyer decides to give up of the deal despite the fact that he already performed due diligence. It might be better to lose 30 000 euros for due diligence than to risk a potential investment of 5 mill euros.

The more prepared you were as a company and the more sincere you were during the negotiations the smaller is the chance that the due diligence can detect an issue which cannot be resolved later on between the two parties. Everybody who is participating in the process know that it is inevitable that some issue will come up. Eventually the people who will conduct that checkup are paid for that. To find problems. That's why the buyer doesn't expect a report which will say that everything is perfect. There are no risks and no problems. The question is what the nature of the problems is and whether they can be solved. No buyer has a goal to find issues or to look for calf under the ox if we can say like that. Nobody has the intention to break up of the deal. So don't worry if some issues arise after the due diligence. If you were honest and have run your accounting according to the tax regulations you will find a solution to the pointed issues.

Types of due diligence

In internet you can find several approaches how you can organize the process of due diligence. According to most experts you can divide it in three big groups: financial, legal, and tax due diligence. In general this is the form which the companies use to submit their offers for providing that service. Sometimes you might have to perform also a technology due diligence if you are buying a technology company and want to get more information about the technology they use. You also might have to do and ecological due diligence if the business is expected to pollute the environment. Anyway, without financial, legal, and tax due diligence you cannot get by. Now I will get into more details for the main areas which are examined during the due diligence process and in the appendix you can find a full check list for a due diligence:

Financial. Since I am a financial guy I always start with that part. Eventually the investor want to check if he will pay a fair price for the company. Here the experts have to check the main financial reports of the company for the last 3-4 years. These are the balance sheet, the income statement, and the cash flow statement. They will also check your account receivable and accounts payables. What is your policy for collecting your receivables? The experts will also examine very carefully all contracts for provided loans and if you are using the accrual approach for registering your expenses. The most important thing is to check if your EBITDA is calculated correctly and if some adjustments has to be made. I will get into more details about the adjustments in a little bit.

Sales and marketing. Here the buyer will want to check who your clients are and what your sales policy is. They examiners will ask for a list of all your major clients and the amount of sales for each of them during the last 2-3 years. How the turnover has changes for a particular client? Is there concentration of sales in several big clients? Analysis of the marking campaigns you have conducted and the sales channels you have used. How effective are they?

Suppliers and inventory. In regards to the suppliers the examiners will also want to see the documents and calculation about the turnover of the main accounts. What are the payment terms? Are you dependable on some suppliers and how your relationship evolve with them during the years? Analysis of your inventory and raw materials stock. What accounting methods you are using for the inventory? What is the policy of the company for choosing new suppliers? They will also check some key contract with the key suppliers.

Real estate. The above three groups we could put under the umbrella of the financial due diligence and now we will switch to the legal part. The first group is the fixed assets which your company owns. The experts will ask for the notary deeds, the contract with which you have acquired the fixed assets, sketches of the properties and the most important thing is if there are some mortgages or other liabilities on these fixed assets.

Intellectual property. This group of assets is becoming more and more important when you are acquiring a company and in some cases it can be the only asset which the company possess. The examiners will ask documents for all patents which your company owns. A list of all domains and registrations which you have. If you have registered brands and trademarks you will have to provide documents for each brand and for each market/country where the brand or the trademark is registered. Their range in terms of time and geography. If you are using software products what are these products and what are the terms you have negotiated for their usage.

Contracts. The due diligence team will want to check all your major contract with suppliers, clients, ownership in subsidiary companies, investment contract, etc. In general all contract which can be of a material interest for the deal.

Company information. Here the experts will check the documents for the registration of your company. For example the articles of incorporation, any increases of the capital, check the shareholders, any changes in the shareholder structure, etc. If your activity requires the usage of some special license they have to be examined. For example for insurance, for banking activities or if you are working in the gambling sector.

Court cases. Here the experts will check all legal cases which your company is involved either as a claimer or as a defendant. If there are pending legal court cases they will estimate what will be the risk to lose these cases and what can be the financial losses or benefits from their outcome.

Human resources. We can form a separate group all checkup which are related to your employees. What is your organizational structure? A full list of your employees with a detail breakdown based on age, education, and how long they have been working for the company. A review of the contracts with the key executives of the company. What is the situation with any unpaid vocations? Do you have signed a collective labor contract? Do you have labor unions in your company? Do you provide additional perks to your employees like food vouchers, additional vocation days, etc.

Tax due diligence. Taxes can turn to be a huge problem and no company can fight with the government successfully. A good example is how the richest man in Bulgaria in 2020 was led to bankruptcy because he got into fight with the government. You can also see the example of Al Capone who was prosecuted for taxes. That's why the examiners will want you to present your tax declarations for the last five years or as long as the tax statute of limitations is in your country. You also has to provide your VAT declarations and the payments of social security of your employees. In general they will check all tax documents and the risk which can arise from not paying all required taxes during the years.

Ecological due diligence. If the activity of the company suggests that it might cause ecological problems and future claims then this subject also has to be examined. In most cases we will be talking for manufacturing companies. What is the company procedure for the waste storage and its processing? Licenses and documents in regards to the usage of water. The storage of any raw materials and finished good especially if they can be hazardous.

Nevertheless if the due diligence takes 30 or 90 days there is no way that the examiners will be able to check all details and documents in the company. However, such checkup will give him some serenity that there will be no major risks and the key items are checked. The investor will receive a detail report from the due diligence team with the problems they have found and what can be the possible outcome of these problems. Based on this report the buyer and the seller has to sit down and see what they can do about these issues and how they can continue the M&A process. If the risks are not significant they can negotiate additional warranties from the side of the seller or can change a little bit the terms of the deal. If the problems are significant and the two parties cannot reach an agreement on them then the investor will pull off from the process. Now the seller will have the option either to contact some of the other interested investors and to propose them to conduct a due diligence on the company or the seller can just cancel the whole procedure. It might turns out that the risks which were identified in the due diligence are objective and they will also be discovered by the other potential investors. There will be no point to invite other investors to do due diligence. It will be better if the company owner to take some time off and try to fix his house. Each company and each process is unique but I will try to summarize the most common problems which are discovered during the due diligence process.

The most common problems discovered during the due diligence

Concentration of clients or suppliers. This is not a reason to cancel the deal but brings additional risk to the buyer and he will like to protect himself in some way

Wrong EBITDA. The formula here is clear and you as a company owner can calculate it very easy. This will happen by taking your profit before taxes add the interest which you have paid for your credits and leasing and at the end also add the depreciation. Nothing complex here. You didn't lie in the number which you have provided as EBITDA to your potential buyers. However the due diligence might reveal that the situation is a little bit different and actually your EBITDA and the profitability of the business are little bit different than the numbers you have provided. What can be the reasons for the adjustments which has to be made to the stated EBITDA? The first reason can be the salary of the owner. Since it is your business very often the company owners don't calculate themselves a normal salary for the position they take. This is usually the executive director of the company. It is normal because the business is yours and it is like to get the money from your left pocket and to put them in your right pocket. That's Ok but lest say that you have a salary of 1000 euros per month and tomorrow I buy your company. There is a huge probability that you will leave the company in several months and I have to find a new CEO which will run the company. He will ask most probably for a salary of 10 000 euros per month. This way instead of the annual expense of 12 000 euros for your salary I will have an expense of 120 000 euros for the new CEO. In this situation the most normal thing is the investor to decrease your EBITDA with 100 000 euros. Unless you find him a new CEO who will agree to run the company for 1000 euros per month. Another possible adjustments might be due to the fact that the company has a significant increase of its revenues because of the sale of an asset. You could also have won some legal case and this year you will have a one-time positive effect in the amount of 500 000 euros which you will not have in the next years. These adjustment cannot be only in negative direction for the company owner. Perhaps it happened the opposite case. You have lost a court case and this year you have paid 500 000 euros and your EBITDA is with 500 000 smaller than it is used to be. In both cases (negative and positive adjustments) you have to analyze all one time effects on the EBITDA. You use this indicator as the base for the company valuation and it implies that this number, all other stuff unchanged, will be the same next year, and the year after that. That's why it is used as a base for the multiplier. In general the idea of the due diligence is to clear out the EBITDA from one time effects.

The due diligence also might find out that you have signed contracts with related companies not on market levels. For example the contracts for the rent of some fixed assets can be on levels which are much lower than the market levels. This will artificially increase your profitability and the net profit. When we talked about the valuation I gave you an idea how you can converge the discrepancies in the valuation between the buyer and the seller. This will happen by taking out the fixed assets into a separate company. The key here is to pay the market rates for the rent. If you don't do it at the moment when the buyer buys the company he might be forced to pay higher rents for the assets because he will not be related anymore to these assets. Sometimes the owners also tend not to report the capital expenditures correctly. Some of the bigger expenses has to be considered capital expenditures and their value has to be added to the value of the machines. Later on through the depreciation they are also taken out from your income. This is the correct approach but it takes longer time. That's why the owner are inclined to consider them operating expenses to deduct them right away form the current profit which saves them more taxes. At the same time this approach can have a negative effect on the valuation because it will decrease the EBITDA for the current year. As you can see the idea of the due diligence is not so much to find problems in your company so that they make you decrease the price but to present the profitability of the company in the most correct way through adjustments to the EBITDA.

Unreal operating itmes related to the revenues of the company. Some of the items we have discussed in the EBITDA issue and the adjustments but here it is another case. Sometimes the company is signing a long term contract (2-3 years) and when they receive the payment they add the whole amount for the first year. The right approach is to use the accrual accounting and to spread the received payment through the three year contract. Not using the accrual approach can lead to a change in the revenues for the current year and from here it will also change the net profit of the company by increasing it.

Sometimes the due diligence reveals missing documents for some of the assets or discrepancies between the documents and the real situation. You have to check all documents to understand why discrepancy takes place. For example in a deal which we recently worked on there was a difference between the notary deed and the sketch of a piece of land. The difference was 20 000 sq m. You as an owner that didn't notice it because you know how much land you using in practice for your activities. Until a person initiate a sale process for an asset, either personal or company owned, he doesn't realize that there might be huge discrepancies in the documentation.

 The company owners. Under this definition I will put all owners of family companies which are an object of a due diligence conducted by the big four auditors. The big four auditors have some rules and procedures which they follow very strictly. In most cases the big four are performing due diligence on the big international companies and their due diligence check list are created in accordance with their way of running business. From time to time an investor hire them to conduct a due diligence on a comparatively small family business. All of a sudden in these case a huge problem shows up with the collection of the necessary data. The auditors will send you a long list with the required documents. You can see an example in the appendixes. When the owner of the family business sees that list and he receives a headache.

It is a very extensive list and the work and the efforts he has to put in order to collect all these information will be significant. Another issue is that sometimes even the auditors cannot check some of the information because it is not based on official documents. On top of everything in most family companies most of the information is in the head of the owner and everything has to go through his hands. During these time when the due diligence last (3-4 months) the owner also has to run his company. In reality he doesn't have the personal recourses to do both activities at the same time and the whole due diligence process is delayed significantly. This very often is perceived by the auditors as a sign that the owner is not so committed to the process and that's how they present it in the report. As a result you can have heated discussion between the investor and the company owner on the progress of the due diligence. The better the company is prepared in the first stage of the M&A process which is the preparation phase then less will be the risk later on in the due diligence process.

The due diligence can reveal that some of the key competences are concentrated in one or two persons. Very often this is the owner and people from his family. It will be necessary to stat a training program and to start "transferring' that knowledge to other key managers in the company. If this doesn't take place the company will remain dependent on that 1-2 persons and will be hard to sell it.

Very often there are missing contracts between the company and its key suppliers or clients. Everything is based on the good will of the two parties and their long term relationship. This situation might be OK for you as an owner but there is no way to be acceptable for the new owner and especially if it is a financial investor. If a problem arise the new owner will not be familiar with the history of that relationships and the only thing they can rely on is written contracts.

The company is in the middle of a big legal case. The lawyers have to check very carefully all documents and the progress so far on the legal case so that they can forecast what the potential risks are for the company in the future if the legal case is lost in the court.

It can turns out that the value of the raw materials and the inventory is overestimated. Perhaps a physical checkup has to be done to see how much of the raw materials and the goods are available in the warehouses and what is the real value. How they are reported on the entrance and on the exit of the warehouse. This can reduce the value of the assets of the company and it is also taken into the valuation.

A huge problem in the due diligence is when there is discrepancies between the data in the official financial statements and the real business data. Any business is trying to cut corners and in the family business it is even more common practice because the owners see the company as their own asset and don't distinguish it much from the personal assets. As we discussed a due diligence is based only on the official documents. There is no way any examination done by outside people to check the real business processes in the company.

As a result of this practice the company owner wants his business to be valued based on the real result because he know that the company is really making 1 200 000 euros net profit not the 1 mill euros which is shown in the official income statement. It is almost impossible for an investor to do it. Then this leads to discrepancies in the valuation and very often the process is cancelled. One option to solve that problem is to make the company valuation based on the official financial statements and that amount to be paid at signing the contract. Afterwards both sides will have one year to take all operations on a white area and if it turns out that the profit really is bigger than the one in the official statements for the last year then the investor will pay additional money to the previous owner. There is no way that all hidden profit will be added to the official profit because in the process of whitening of the financials some of it will be lost for tax purposes or other reasons. Well, this is the price which you as an owner have to pay for conducting your business not according to the normal business practices. The good news is that there is a way how to solve that problem if there is a will in both parties.

Another problem in the due diligence phase is the communication between the two parties. Besides the seller, the buyer and their consultants, now in the process will be involved also lawyers, auditors and tax experts. All of them will look at the issue from their own perspective and believe that the issues which they are in charge are the most crucial one for the whole deal. Here comes the important role of the M&A consultant to control the process and remind all involved parties what the main goal of the whole operation is. It is to close the deal because the seller and the buyer have invested a lot in the process so far and they have reached an agreement on the deal terms. The rest participants might not have the same interest because they are paid by an hours and they are interested to put more hours in the process so that they can get a bigger remuneration. That's why you have to be careful that somebody from the due diligence team can take himself for the leading actor in the whole show.

In my opinion the process of due diligence is a little bit overvalued when we are talking for family owned businesses. First of all if you have a small business or just selling assets there is no need of due diligence. If you are selling a stake in the company both parties should be correct to each other because they will have to work together after the deal. We also discussed why the executives of the strategic buyers and the investment funds are performing due diligence. They are right to request it and there are benefits form that step. My 15 years experience shows me that in most cases if there is a problem which comes up after the deal most probably it cannot be found based on checking the documentation of the company. A due diligence process does exactly that. Check the documents of the company. A better, faster and much cheaper alternative to the extensive due diligence is to sit down and see what warranties the investor wants from the seller. The seller knows very well what the real situation of the company is and if he knows that everything is OK then he should not have any problems to take on bigger warranties about the deal. They will protect the investor from finding any skeletons in the wardrobe as is the jargon in the M&A sector.

Closing the deal

We are really now at the final stage of the process of selling your business. The due diligence went well or at least you have solved the issue which were brought by it and now it is time to close the deal. The bigger part of the steps which have to be taken here will be a duty of your lawyers. Although you are at the final stage you still can encounter hidden problems and unfortunately I had a case where the deal didn't close just because the lawyers couldn't agree under which jurisdiction will be signed the final contract. The buyer was a big American public company and their lawyers requested to apply the Anglo-Saxonian law. At the same time the lawyers of the Bulgarian company insisted the contract to be govern under the Bulgarian legislation. There might have been also other differences between the two parties but at least the official version for not signing the deal was the jurisdiction. As a result although everything was negotiated, the due diligence checked OK, the deal was not closed. That's why you don't have to celebrate yet and you must pay attention to the technical aspects which has to be taken in this phase. A deal is closed officially when the money are in your bank account.

The main document which has to be prepared at this stage is the final contract which is also known as SPA (Share purchase agreement). Your lawyers can prepare a draft of the contract which you can send to the buyer or vice versa. If you prepare the draft you have to pay more money to your lawyers because they have to prepare the draft. However the draft will be written in a favorable way for you. If the buyer offers you a draft of the contract you will save some money for lawyers but most probably you will spend more time to renegotiate some of the clauses since they will be written in favor of the buyer. If you have negotiated with your lawyers a package price for the whole process then it will be better they prepare the draft. I will not get into details how such contract should look like because neither I, neither you, are lawyers but I will point out the main topics which has to be included in the document:

Parts of the SPA (Share Purchase agreement)

The names of the buyer and the seller. Their location, the name and some data for the company

The assets which will be sold. Are we talking for specific assets or for shares of the company. What percentage of the shares will be transferred? The amount which will be paid by the buyer. Will there be a capital increase and issuing new shares or the buyer will acquire existing shares (cash out deal).

What liabilities will be taken by the new owner? For example the existing bank loans will be taken by the buyer or the seller has to paid them in advance and transfer the company with no financial liabilities.

The date when the deal will be closed

What will be the form of the payment? When the money will be transferred? Will the buyer pay the whole agreed amount in a lump sum or there will several payments? Will they use ESCROW account? Since I used this term several times let me explain what it means. This is a special type of bank account which is used as an intermediary step. To some extend I can compare it to a letter of credit. For example the buyer deposits the money in the ESCROW account and they are not anymore in his possession. However the money are still not in your possession either. Only the bank is in power and can manage the money. When you open such account the two parties also sign a special ESCROW agreement which implicitly states the terms under which the bank can release the whole amount or part of it to the seller. With this instrument you can solve the trust problem between the two parties. Part of the money can stay into this account for some time to cover some of the warranties which the seller has given to the buyer. This is a normal practice in the more complex deal.

The legislation according to which future disputes between the two parties will be solved in the court.

The personal agreements with the company owner. Very often when you are selling a majority stake or 100% of your company the buyer will require you to sign an agreement that you will not develop a similar business for some period of time. The so called non-compete agreement. There is always a fear in the buyers that after the deal is closed you might be tempted to start a similar business. You know the industry and have relationships with most suppliers and clients. It will be very easy for you to launch a new company and try to "steal" some of the business of your ex company. That's why in most cases the buyer will ask you to sign such agreement. It is another topic how easy it is to apply such agreement in some countries. For example if you have decided to start a competing business it will be hard for the buyer to stop you. You will not formally be the owner or the executive of the new company, which can be owned by the cousin of your uncle, but in practice you run it. In general if a person wants to cheat and to deceive another person it will be hard for any formal agreements to stop him. These people are very creative in the ways how to cut some corners in the business.

The date according to which the new owner has to measure the level of the inventory and the working capital in the company. When we talked about the valuation of the company I mentioned that the cash in the bank account will stay usually in the seller. On the other side the working capital is part of the business and it is included in the transaction. That's why some company owners can be tempted to decrease the level of working capital in the company and to increase the cash. This happens by pushing to receive the money from the accounts receivables and also delaying the payments of the accounts payables.

The additional cash which will be released form that operations can be added to the rest cash in the company and to be paid to the seller. Because of that risk the two parties in advance calculate what the normal level of working capital in the company is and it is written in the contract. At the moment of the transfer of the ownership the working capital should be at least at that level.

Warranties and representations by the company owner. Here the lawyers includes clauses such as; you are the owner of the assets which are sold, the information which you have given the buyer is the truth, you are not aware of other liabilities besides the ones which you already revealed to the buyer, etc. You have to declare also that you have paid all necessary taxes. You have submitted all requested information, contracts, license for the normal operating of the business. In other words you declares that you have been honest till now in the whole process and you didn't hide and deceive any information in the due diligence and the whole M&A process.

Warranties and representations on the side of the buyer. Here the buyer declares that he has the authority to execute the deal.

An agreement for the transfer of the business. The seller is obliged to transfer all necessary contracts such as: rent of some assets, leasing contracts, intellectual property, an agreement with the bank that the bank doesn't mind the mortgage assets to become in possession of the new owner. This will apply if you have agreed that the buyer will take over the bank loans of the company.

 Sometimes the two parties also include a clause for the participated M&A consultants and how they will be compensated for their work so there is no risk that they will look for their compensation from the company itself not from the seller.

Most probably I have missed some key elements of the SPA but let's leave it to the lawyers. There are a couple more key elements which you have to agree on before you sign the contract. One of them is whether you have to request an approval from the commission for protection of the competition. In the different countries it might have different names. For some deals this formal act can be a break dealer. In Bulgaria we had two recent cases when the government decided not to approve the sale of the biggest TV program to one investor but allowed to be sold to a different one. Similar cases we have also in Western Europe and in the USA. It concerns mainly some acquisitions by Chinese companies. If your company is not of a national importance even if the formal requirements require an approval of the regulatory bodies you shouldn't worry about it. However, from a formal point of view you have to wait for the approval of the regulatory bodies before officially close the deal. In each country the requirements of such approval might differ but I will post you the requirement in Bulgaria which as an EU member should be pretty much similar to the ones in other EU countries. According to the law in Bulgaria these are the cases when you should require an approval. If your company doesn't fall in any of these case then you don't even have to ask for such approval.

The effect of the concentration of the two companies will be insignificant when the total share of the combines services or product of the two companies doesn't exceed:

10% market share if the two companies are competitors
15% of each segment if the two companies are not competitors

Another key point is to decide which legal entity will actually will acquire your company. Bulgaria is a country with very low taxes. We have 10% corporate tax and 10% flat personal income tax. When the deal is let's say 10 mill euros despite the low taxes the owner still won't be so happy to pay 1 mill in taxes. If the deal is in the USA, France or in Scandinavia where the taxes are so much higher the owner will be even more motivated to do something which can help him to save some taxes. There are some offshore zones which allows you to optimize your income for tax purposes. For example the Netherlands, Malta and some islands. I am not an expert in this field and not to mislead you I will advise you to get consultation form a tax expert about this issue. What I know from my experience is that if you decide to make use of that practice then you have to launch this process of tax optimization as soon as possible. You cannot register an offshore company one month before the deal is executed and to hope to benefit in full extend from the tax evasion opportunities. It will be too obvious why are you doing it and the tax authorities will not approve it.

What will happen if you have breached some of the warranties you have given to the buyer? In general the two parties always leave some amount money in the ESCROW account for at least a year. When the buyer finds out that you have acted in bad faith the buyer has two options. He can compensate himself with the money in the ESCROW account. If the amount is not enough then he can file a legal case in the court to cover his losses. This is a final measure and it will take a long time in order to get some compensation but it is still an option for the buyer. However the first option with ESCROW account is easy to be executed and you as a company owners won't have much to do in order to stop him. Because of that any buyer would like to have bigger amount hold in the ESCROW account and for longer time. As a company owner you will have the opposite desire. The amount to be minimal for a maximum of 6-12 months. Another common case when the seller has to put some money in the ESCROW account is for tax purposes. They will stay as a warranty there in case there are claims from the government if it conduct a tax examination of the company. Very often the parties put a clause that if a tax inspection is conducted and no major problems are detected then the bigger part of the money in the ESCROW account is released to the seller.

On the appointed date and time together with your lawyers, shareholders, and sometimes your spouses you go to the notary office to sign the deal. You will have to sign some papers there. You also have to appoint a shareholder meeting where a new board of directors will be chosen and a new CEO. All these changes also has to be published in the commercial register so that everything is official. You also have to foresee the following action on your side so that the new owner can easy and fast get into real possession of the new assets or the company:

The code for the alarm systems
Information and contact details of key suppliers and clients
The keys for the office, the cars, and for other assets
To agree on the channel how you will receive the information in case of future problems or steps which has to be taken according to the signed warranties and representations
Submission of all documents like notary deeds etc. Some of the documents the owners keep in their houses instead of the company office.
The insurance policies
The access code and passwords to various software products which the company uses

Everything described so far in the chapter is related to the case when you are selling the whole business. If you are selling only a stake of the company and a new shareholder is included in the shareholder structure then most of these steps won't be necessary. You will continue to run the company together with the new business partner. If this is the case you have to specify how the payment will take place and what the money will be used for. You also have to agree on clauses which are typical when you sell a stake to a financial investor. In general these are questions like: what you will do in three or five years? Who will sell and who will lead the future sale? How you can separate as business partners if some events happen, etc.

At the end you also has to think about the way you will let know all stakeholders in the company about the deal. In the first place these are your employees. It is very likely that they suspect already that something like that happened. Any change brings uncertainty and that's why it will be a good step if you, together with the new owner, organize a meeting with all employees. There you can explain why you are undertaking this step and what will happen from now on. Very often the change in the ownership is for the good of the company and the employees but the uncertainty makes people nervous. The same exercise you have to repeat with your suppliers and clients. Most probably the banks will already know because if you had credits you should have received their approval in advance. Last but not least is the society.

Here it also matters who the buyer is. If it is a public company it is obliged to reveal some information including the amount of the transaction. That's was the case with one of the deals we did with a Polish buyer. At the moment we signed the preliminary contract the Polish investor released a press release on their stock exchange with the key deals parameters. If the deal is between private entities it depends on you if you will release any information about the transaction. The most sensitive info is about the deal amount. Sooner or later people will find out about the deal so it won't be a bad move if you prepare a press release and send it the media with the information you decide to include. If you the owner of a restaurant or an auto body shop it is clear that the society is not so interested in your business and there is no need of press release. You are the person which will decide what information to release.

After closing – integration of the company

The strange thing is that even if you have closed the deal and have received the money still the process might not be over for you as an owner. The nature of some of the M&A deals is selling a stake to a financial investor with the idea for a faster growth or for example one of the shareholders is buying the stake of the other shareholder. If you have a transaction with a strategic buyer still the deal can be structured in several stages. For example the French DPD bought the second biggest Bulgaria courier company Speedy but first they bought 20% and in several years they bought the rest. Even if you have sold 100% of your company to a strategic investor you still might have an earn-out scheme in place and follow up payments. It is very likely that you will have a management contract and an obligation to stay in the company for at least a year and to help for the smooth transition in the ownership. Because of all these reasons the option to sell your business and the next day to go on vocation to a nice warm island is actually a very seldom option. It applies mostly in the cases when you have sold assets not a business.

Actually if you look at the statistics from various researches on the M&A transactions you will find out that around 70% of the M&A deals are defined as unsuccessful. What the authors in these research have in mind is not that the buyers are losing money, although this also happens, but the fact that the buyers cannot make use of the synergies they have planned when they were working on the transaction. A lot of the clients we have talked to have asked me why is that happening? Sometimes the buyer has paid too much money for the company. Sometimes the seller didn't reveal all problems and in later stage the new owner got surprised by unexpected problems. These are all possible cases but the main reason is what is happening in the acquired firm after the deal. It's integration in the business of the investor. That process of integration turned out to be a complex topic and lately it receives more and more attention from the managers and the experts in the field. All participants in the transaction have an interest to increase the effectiveness from the merger of both companies.

Even the seller is interested. If the integration is not happening according to the plan it is likely that the company will worsen its financial results. As a result most probably the seller will not receive the full amount of the follow up payments it has negotiated during the deal. That's why you as company owners also should care what will happen after the deal is closed. You have a financial interest to participate actively in the integration process and to help the new owner to make the transition smoothly. Sometimes you can be even the buyer in an M&A deal and in next chapter we will talk about that topic.

Very often the experts define the M&A deals as the marriage between a man and a woman. You have two separate organizations with different corporate culture, different processes and procedures. On top of that they have to learn to live together. While you are negotiating the deal all indications show that it makes perfect sense for the merger and there will be a lot of synergies. Eventually as everybody knows about 50% of all marriages ends up with a divorce and people are surprised why it happened when the two newly wed looked destined to be together. For example you have spent a lot of time to court your future wife. You went out together or in other words you have done due diligence on her. Finally you decided to get married and in several years it turns out that things will not work out between you.

One of the main reasons for that discrepancy in the mergers & acquisitions is that the focus during the whole transaction is too short-term. All participants in the process are doing their best in attempts to present the company in the best possible way in order to receive the maximum value. If you the buyer you tried to find as many flows as possible so that you decrease the price. The financial investors know how difficult process is the integration of a company or how difficult the ownership transition process is. To protect themselves, since they are chasing annual yield, they are trying to buy the companies as cheap as possible. This way even if the integration of the company doesn't go by plan they still might have room not to lose money. They just have bought it very cheap. However, the fund managers not always can buy companies under the market value. It happens usually when the owners are pressed to the wall for some reason. One of the shareholders had died or the owner has to sell the company very fast for personal reasons. In most deals the paid price by the investor is the fair market value. The upside from the deal will come from the future development of the business.

Actually, when I think now a significant part of the foreign investments in Eastern Europe are Greenfield investments. Yes, sometimes the local owners want a price which is way too high in the eyes of the foreign investors but a big factor in favor of the Greenfield investments is the lack of integration of an existing business. When a foreign investor buys your company you already have established processes and rules how to run the company. Most probably they differ from investor's way of doing business. Sometimes these differences are of objective nature. For example the size of the business. It is one way how to manage a company with 100 employees and a completely different approach is to manage an organization with several thousand employees and several locations. Besides you know how different the people are. It is one way how the anglo-soxonian people do business and it is completely different how the people in Southern Europe are doing business. So, is it for objective or subjective reasons the different management styles are a fact. Imagine that you have used to work in a certain way and tomorrow somebody comes and tells you that from tomorrow you have to perform your task in a completely different way. It is normal to show some resistance especially if the communication from the new owner was not very effective. Why does he wants you do perform your task in a completely different way? A friend of mine who was a coach in Volleyball once told me: "I prefer to have a kid which has never played volleyball and I can teach him from scratch instead of to have a kid which was taught to play in the wrong way".

Management is not math and it is hard to say which of the two styles of management the better one is. For sure the new style will be different from what you have used to. In such situation the buyer has to think very carefully and to act slowly. Not to make big changes from the very beginning. I can give you an example with one confectionary factory in Bulgaria which was bought by a Private equity fund. The deal was structured in such way that the owners acquired right away 90% of the company from the two founders. As a result the fund also had to take over the management. Before the deal and after the deal the company was a great business which was making several million euros net profit. The two founders had these great results without using any aggressive marketing, any business plans, no written procedures and rules. They were everyday in the company and have built it from scratch. From the moment they were the only employees to the moment to have 500 employees and 30 mill euros sales. As I like to say they manage the business as craftsmen. I don't imply anything negative in that definition and you can run a company this way and to make good money. However, you will have two problems.

First the business cannot grow too much because it is limited to the resources which the founders have as personal time. The second problem is that the company is very dependable on the founders. The PE fund as well the other financial investors which were researching the company saw in that situation an opportunity. They were thinking that if they bring an experienced CEO from a multinational company and apply an aggressive marketing strategy which is normal for the FMCG companies they would double the sales of the Bulgarian factory. They brought in one Greek guy who used to work for Nestle and the things didn't work out well. I cannot say what the real reasons were because I was not inside of the company but if a person checks the financial results of the company in the first years after the transaction he will see a decrease in the sales and especially in the net profit. It is one way to manage a big company with an established corporate structure as Nestle and a completely different thing to manage a big Bulgarian company which is actually a family business in its structure.

After the first shock the fund managers realized that they made a mistake and they hired a Bulgarian manager. As far as I can see it is doing well now. I haven't checked if the company surpassed its financial results compared to the moment when the fund bought it but I know that it managed to establish some corporate structure and now the company is more prepared to be sold to a foreign multinational company and it is not so dependent on its CEO. Because of that now the fund will have easier task to sell it to another company from the sector or even bigger financial investor because the new owner will not experience anymore these problems related to the transition from a family business (craftsman) to a corporation. Actually this will be more the case when the buyer is again a financial investor because then there will not be much change. Any strategic buyer will have a unique style and might make changes but still the transition phase will be much easier than in the first deal.

When you have a strategic investor the problem can be even bigger. Of course it depends on the reason why they have bought the company in the first place. Sometimes the buyers wants just the clients of the acquired company.

The investor has enough production capabilities and they will transfer the clients to other locations. In 2-3 years they can shut down the local company which they have bought. Another case is when they just want a production place with low manufacturing costs. Nothing of the management processes is of importance. They will just manufacture in Bulgaria. The marketing, the finance, sales and all other administrative functions will be performed from abroad. I can give you an example with a company from 15 years ago. Because the company doesn't exist anymore so I can reveal names. So we had a top three Bulgarian juice producer (BBB juices) and a big Austrian buyer, which also from the same sector. The Austrian company wanted to buy the Bulgarian firm but the Bulgarian owner asked for such price that the owner of the Austrian company told him: "Look we have a very strong brand. We also have good sales in Bulgaria. I just don't want to bring the juice from 1000 km. but to produce them locally. So I just need the production facilities. With the money you asked from me I can build two brand new factories instead of buying your business". They couldn't agree on the price and the deal didn't take place. However if they agreed on the price the integration in this case would be much easier because the new owner wouldn't have to integrate the administration process of the two companies. He would just have a production facility in Bulgaria.

The integration process is hardest when you have two similar business and you want to integrate them into one whole. For example you can have two banks or as we had the case of one Bulgarian company which was producing rain gutters, which we sold to a Polish investor from the same sector. The investor from Poland was a strategic buyer and they sold their products in the upper price segment. On the other side the Bulgarian company was selling the product in the lower prices segments. The Polish investor wanted to use that fact and with the acquisition to enter the low price segment of the retail store chains "Do it yourself" The strategy sounded very logical and made sense. So the Polish guys bought 100% of the Bulgarian company and the Bulgarian owners left the company completely. I cannot say how the integration took place but I can see that the financial results of the Bulgarian subsidiary in the first 2-3 years after the deal were lower than the financial results the company had before the deal.

Because of all these examples I gave you and I am sure that they are representative for any country, any experienced buyer is very concerned about the transition period after the deal is signed. If the current owner is OK to stay in the company for 1-2 years and he is also ready to bind the company price with some earn-out scheme and follow up payments it will be a key factor for the signing of the deal. On the other side it is completely understandable that the current owners are not so happy with that scheme. On one side they have to be responsible for the financial results of the company in the next 1-2 years and on the other side they cannot take all decision by themselves. For example sometimes the new owner is taking decision from the whole group perspective and sometimes it will be good for the whole group to transfer profits from one client to another location. He is not looking only from the local Bulgarian perspective. At the same time you might not be happy about this policy because you care only for the results of the Bulgarian division and your bonuses depends mainly on the results of the Bulgarian division. Let aside the fact that in the first place most probably you sold the company because you were tired. Now all of a sudden you sold the company but you still have to work hard the next 1-2 years to earn your follow up payments. Here comes again the question about the motivation. Is it better to chase a maximum price but then have to agree to this earn-out scheme or you can sell at a lower price but leave the business the next day after the signing?

In the process of integration the experience of the buyer is of key importance. Has he done already similar deals and does he know what exactly happens after signing the deal? If it is expected from you to stay in the company for some period then both sides have to write down in details what exactly you are supposed to do, what will be your responsibilities and your rights. It will be useful for you if you check and see if the buyer had gone through such process already. If they have done it then they will know what mistakes they have done in the past and this time they will be much more careful. If it is their first time they can act a lot more arrogant. They are the people who calls the shots now and can jeopardize the smooth transition of the change in the ownership.

There are a several key items which stay in the base of the integration expenses for both parties in the process. In the first group we can put the expenses related to your employees. Their departure and the loss of key competences inside the firm can lead to additional expanses and missed opportunities for the company. Besides, your employees might have to acquire new competences since they will have to work with new clients, new procedures, new software, etc. It will require some training. That's why after each deal the training expenses and the hiring expenses are the major item in the integration budget. We also mentioned that after each change it is normal to have some stress among the employees. Even if you as an owner stay in the company the employees know that now there is a new person in charge and a lot of rumors will start spreading around. You will try to calm the employees down that everything will run like in the old days and there is nothing they have to worry about but while they don't see it in practice there will be some concerns. Each employee who is put in such situation will have three major questions in front of him.

Do I still have a job?
Whom I have to report to and who is my direct boss?
How much and how I will be paid?

That's' why your first task, together with the new owner, is to address these three questions in front of all employees.

It has to be your first priority. If you stop the speculation and calm down your employees you would have made a huge step in the successful change in ownership and will minimize the expenses related to the employees. For some businesses this might be the main asset. Imagine that you are an IT company. Somebody buys you and within the next 6 months 20% of your employees leave and go to your competitors. Even if you manage to replace them this process will lead to some turmoil and there is huge probability to lose some of your clients. The clients are used in practice to work with your employees not with the company per se.

The second big item for the integration expenses is related to the IT systems. In 2004 I was working for a local bank which was bought by another bank. I saw it personally how the integration of the software turned into a big problem. In my bank they have just installed a new banking software and several months afterwards a deal was signed. The buyer, the other bank, was using completely different software and vendor for the same application. Now they had to implement their software in our bank. Everybody who had something to do with integration of an ERP system or some type of software knows that in practice it always takes a lot longer time and a lot more money than it is planned in the beginning. If the two organization are comparatively the same size it doesn't mean that the change always has to be in one direction. Everything which is in the buyer organization to be implemented in the target organization.

Sometimes it might be better to take the ERP system of

the target and to implement it in the organization of the buyer. If the buyer has an established corporate structure with rules and procedures it will be much easier and cheaper the change to happen there. The goal is both companies to work with the same software system so that there is a synchrony but which it will be it not so important. That of course is true if we assume that both software systems are of equal qualities. Just different brands. It is hard to say which car is better? Mercedes or BMW, right? It is clear that one of the parties have to learn to drive the other car but who is an open question. Moreover this step can be a very good sign for the employees in the acquired company that the goal of the management is really to merge the two companies into one family. Not the buyer to treat you as a "colony". This happens very often in some companies even if there is no integration process because of a merger. You know very well how the people in the HQ treat the people in the subsidiaries. Very often as second rate people.

As specific steps which you have to take in the integration process we can point out the following actions:

There are some technical stuff which we have discussed in the previous chapter as giving access to passwords, e-mails, access to software, etc

It is the responsibility of the buyer to form a team or at least to appoint a person who will be in charge of the process of the integration of the two companies. This will not be a formal position in the hierarchy but more of a project manager who will directly be subordinated to the owner/CEO of the buyer. That project manager will also directly work with you. If you are still involved in the operating activates of the company it will be in your personal interest to help that project manager. You still have bonuses to receive, right?

What goals have been set and what is the timeframe for their achievement? How the achievement of each goal will affect the company business and what changes has to be made? In general the bigger the changes which has to be made the bigger the turmoil which you can expect and bigger integration expenses you will have.

Have clear rules for the communication in the new organization. Who with whom can communicate directly in the new merged organization. It is normal practice when you have a family business for almost all issues the final saying to be that of the owner. If you are becoming part of a big corporation this will not be like that and it will be good if it is explained to your employees.

There should be a clear procedure how the conflicts in the organization will be addressed and solved. Till now perhaps the final problem solver was you as the owner of the company but this has to be changed.

You as the owner of the acquired company has to be clear that from now most probably the formal procedures will increase or as I call them the bureaucracy in the organization. It is normal for a big organization to have a lot of rules, written procedures, reports, etc. You as an entrepreneur can think that this is pointless and it is just a waste of time but there is no other way to manage a big company. That's' why you have to be prepared to start writing reports every week. I talk from time to time with some owners which companies were acquire by big international corporation and ask them how the things are. One of the first things they tell me is that they turned into "writers" and every week have to write reports to the HQ. This new practice you have to spread in your company down to the lower levels of administration. If you don't do it then for real you will be writing reports for everything. Even for the stuff which shouldn't be your direct responsibility.

 Most probably you will have to eliminate some duplicating processes and departments and to lay off some people. If the benefit is obvious the sooner you do it the better will be for everybody. You just have to do it based on objective criteria and people will understand you.

The processes and the problems I described in this chapter are typical for any organization all over the world. If a family company in Germany or in Italy is working as a craftsman organization the buyers there will have similar problems to what I have seen in Eastern Europe. That's why the statistics say that 70% of the M&A transaction cannot realize the synergies they have planned to in the beginning. This statistics is for the whole world. So you cannot say that in some regions people are not so smart, don't know what to do and that's why the deals fail.

In the developed countries they also have the same problem. As it is in most cases the knowledge comes with the experience and the experience comes with the mistakes. In Eastern Europe we still don't have many M&A deals and that's why it is normal to make more mistakes because we didn't make enough mistakes to learn from. At the end of the chapter I have to say that if you sold just assets or have received the whole payment for your business at the signing of the deal then you can miss the whole chapter. The problems I described will be totally for the new owner. Unless you are thinking to buy another business. We will talk about that opportunity in the next chapter. In this case this integration process will be your biggest concern.

Buying a business

Till now we talked mainly for the option that one day you will sell a part or whole your business. Actually in order to have a deal you must have a buyer. As many people are selling their business the same amount of people should be buying companies. I don't know why when I am talking about mergers and acquisitions most people think that by default they should sell their business. There are several reasons for that phenomenon in the Eastern European countries. Some of them are objective but others are subjective. For my 15 years M&A practice I can say that around 90% of our projects have been related to the sale of a company and only in 10% of the assignment our clients were buying another business. Bulgaria is a small country and our companies are comparatively small in terms of the international standards. That's why it is not easy for their owners to go out on the international market and to compete with the big international companies when there is an option to buy another company.

Besides the perception of our entrepreneurs is that the normal path is they to set up some type of business, develop it to a certain point and then to sell it to a foreign company. There is nothing wrong with that strategy but it doesn't imply that you also can buy an established company. For me the two biggest reasons why most family owned business don't buy so often other companies are of completely different nature. Not so much the size and the location. I believe that most of them are intimidated to go out on the international market and to buy a company in Germany or in the USA. I have seen some deals of that nature but I really can count them on the fingers of my two hands. It is much more often when a Bulgarian company decided to expand abroad to look around for targets in the neighboring countries or in countries which are not so developed as economy. I guess from a psychological point of view if the country is not so developed the owners assume that buyer should be a big company and to come from a more developed country. If the Germans are buying companies in Bulgaria, then the Bulgarian companies can buy businesses in Moldova for example. The problem is that these companies, since they are located in less developed countries, most probably are not so well structured and without established corporate structure. As a result most probably after the deal you will have much higher integration cost and a bigger probability that the deal will turn unsuccessful because transformation of ownership failed. If you buy a company in Germany most probably in terms of transparency and established business processes the things will be much better than what you can find in an average company in Serbia or in Moldova.

Most probably also the price which you will pay in regards to the financial results of the company will also be much better. It is a paradox that it is much easier to find a good company in Germany which you can buy for 4-5 times EBITDA than you can do it in Eastern Europe. For a long time the multiple of EBITDA in Eastern Europe were very high and every owner was expecting that he can sell his company for 7-10 times EBITDA. The reason behind this logic was the assumption that Eastern Europe is developing market and here the forecast for the expected growth was very good. In general experts expected a lot of potential for growth. At the same time the developed markets were saturated with a lot of competitors and that's why the expectations for growth on this market were not very optimistic. The statistics reveals that a huge part of these expectations for the growth in Eastern Europe were not justified to its full extend and that's why it was unreasonable to pay higher multiples for growth. I would advise any entrepreneur not to be intimidated and look boldly for opportunities for acquisitions on the developed markets.

The second reason not to have so many acquisitions from family businesses is the lack of corporates structure in their businesses.

Actually the entrepreneurs are making deals but mostly for assets not live businesses. In order to be able to manage one company from distance (another location) then those businesses should be able to operate without your everyday presence in the firm. If you haven't achieved that status with your business then there is no way that you can do apply in the business which you will acquire. Yes, the business in your company is doing very well and you are making good profit. The question is if everything will continue the same way if you buy a company in Spain and now you have to spend a lot of time in Spain to integrate the new business. For me this is the main reason why the owners of the family businesses in Bulgaria and I assume also in other countries are afraid to buy a business in a foreign country. Actually I didn't want to say that the acquired business have to be in a foreign country. It can be in your country but in different location. Whether you have to travel 4 hours by car to the other location or 3 hours by plane it doesn't make much difference. Well the culture will be different but the key problem again is whether you have to be physically present in the new business every day. Earlier in the book I gave you the example with the owner of one restaurant who wanted to expand and set up a chain of restaurants. You are very good chef and your restaurant is very profitable.

At the moment when you open a couple other restaurants the picture changes completely. Based on these facts now I understands why most deals in Bulgaria are for acquisition of assets not for whole companies. There is nothing bad in that. When there is an option I would always recommend to buy assets instead of the whole business. This way you can save the cost for due diligence and the risk from the unsuccessful integration of the company after the closure. I assume everybody will agree that if he has the option to buy just the assets (cherry picking of the assets) and leave all liabilities to the current owner that would be best option for each investor. You can sign new contract with the employees and the managers and they will transfer to the new legal entity on the next day. With such scheme it can turns out that there won't be much difference if you bought the legal entity (the company) or you bought the assets. If you also buy the brand and transfer all contracts with the clients and the suppliers nobody will care of the

Company identification number is the same or not. The option with the acquisition of just the assets and leaving the liabilities to the current owner is the best case scenario for any investor but the question is if this is Ok for the seller. In most cases that scheme is applicable if you have a business which has financial difficulties and then it will be better off to sell the assets and at least to return some of the money to its creditors. Another possible case is if a small company is not managed so well and basically its value is higher as assets than in terms of cash flows. But it will be impossible to find a good profitable company like Mercedes or SAP, to buy just the assets and to leave the liabilities of its current owners.

Why should I by an established company?

This is the main question which any entrepreneur has to answer before he launches the acquisition process. At the beginning each of you will have two options. Either you can start your business from scratch as most probably you have started your current business or to buy an established company. Both options have their advantages and disadvantages. Since so many acquisitions take place all over the world there should be some reasons to make sense people to choose that option. Let's get into more details about the main reasons why you should buy an established company:

 You will have something ready right away. Nowadays it is much easier a person to register a company and to start a new business compared to 20-30 years ago. I personally set up two startups in the last five years (you can read about that in my other book about startups) and from a personal experience can confirm that the necessary money to launch a technological startup nowadays are minimal. Startups can use also a lot of free resources for hosting, marketing tools and so many other things. At the same time the competition nowadays is so fierce that the probability your startup to survive after the first 2-3 years is much smaller than it used to be. I have talked to a lot of entrepreneurs about the way how they launched their business in the 90s of last century. I mean the entrepreneurs form Eastern Europe which started private business after the communism. Pretty much none of them was prepared to be an entrepreneur and didn't have the necessary knowledge and skills. They were just braver than the rest of the people and were not afraid to try.

They have launched and since there was still nothing on the market everybody could make money as long as he is more resourceful and persistent. Now to be brave is not enough. You also need some knowledge, skills, and financial resources in order to compete with the big giants like Amazon and Facebook. Some of the current entrepreneurs are feeling that process and that's why they are looking to sell their companies because it is getting harder and harder to compete with the multinational corporations. You can ask the owners of the food retail stores in Eastern Europe what happened after the so called modern trade entered the market. These giants not only know what to do but they also have the financial resource to work some time at a loss just to take the market share from you and to kick out of the market. A good example are the food retail chains. In regards to that if you buy already an established company the risk to go bankrupt is much smaller because it already survived the initial years which are the riskiest.

When you buy an established company you will have from day one a cash flow which will enter you bank accounts. This happens because you bought a profitable company. This fact also make the process of acquiring a company easier because the banks will be ready to provide you more financing for the acquisition. You don't have to believe that in order to buy a company you must have the whole amount ready in cash in your safe. Even if you are buying an apartment it is normal practice to use bank loan to pay a part of the price. For buying a working company it is even more normal because on the first day after the deal you will have 5 euro revenues which you can use to pay back part of the loan.

When you are buying a business you will acquire right away new clients and markets. Perhaps you have heard many times when foreign companies come to you country their managers to say that they are not interested in your building and machines. They are only interested in your clients because this is what brings revenues to any company. Many of the clients are loyal to the brand or to the location and it is not so easy to steal them form the current owner. Even just for the habit they have which is a big obstacle for any change in the human actions. You know that you as an user when you get used to a certain brand or product and you don't experience any significant problems most probably you won't switch it even if something much cheaper or better comes out on the market. In that situation the new company either has to invest a lot of money and resources to "steal" that client or it can just acquire the brand/the company. If the company chooses the first option it might take some time. Even if you have a lot of money sometimes this change doesn't happen.

It might be even impossible to happen. Let's go back to the example with the food retail chains. In that business of key importance is the location of the store. Ok. But most probably all good locations for new stores are already taken in the city where you live. It is becoming harder and harder for the retail chains to find good locations and to open new stores. Many of these companies have aggressive marketing strategies and their business module suggests that they have to reach certain scale in order to be profitable. If you are in such situation then the only option for you to grow as a company is to acquire some of your competitors. Perhaps you don't like their business and you can change it completely but you need the location.

 Economies of scale. For some businesses this is of significant importance and in order their business model to be profitable they have to achieve some level of operations. It is the same even with the social networks. They call it network effect. In the traditional business the scale is also important. I have talked to the owners of several cosmetics companies in Bulgaria and discussed what the situation is. Now the technology is developing and the machines are becoming more and more effective. When you have the scale you can buy a modern machines which can produce thousands of toothpastes per hour.

You can switch on the machines and run it in long series for a certain product. This way despite the higher expenses for salaries the manufactures can produce toothpastes with lower cost structure than a smaller manufactures can do it in a country in Eastern Europe, where the salaries are lower.

You could ask yourself then why if their COGS is lower their prices are higher. It is because of the marketing expenses which the multinational invest in building their brand. The scale also can give you advantages when you negotiate with your suppliers to buy raw materials. Everybody who is running a business know how many advantages the bigger companies have. That's why by buying other business you can become bigger and your business can become more effective and profitable. Now I recall one of our first projects we worked on about 15 years ago. I remember how at that time we had many small cable operators in Bulgaria. The prices for the clients were low because of the fierce competition and the cable operators hardly were making any money. The idea was that somebody have to make a consolidation in the sector. To become big enough so that he can have a significant power and to increase the prices to the end users. Since they wouldn't have much choice the users couldn't do much. This happened in practice and it started from Cabletel which was bought by a PE fund and later on the fund started consolidation on the market by buying their competitors.

This strategy was going to work but the technology developed and new types of alternatives show up. A satellite television where we have a very big player and also the telecom operators started offering also TV services. However a person couldn't forecast that 15 years ago. Basically the economies of scale has always been a big factor when acquisition decision are taken. The biggest companies are making most acquisitions and it is not a coincidence that the regulators are talking about limiting the concentration.

The availability of synergies and cross-selling options. For many business there is an opportunity if they merge their operations with a competitor to realize synergies in their activities. This can lead to reduction in their expenses or to increase in the revenues. For example two banks merge and there will be no need to have two HR departments or two IT teams. At the same time you have twice more clients and this have to lead to a bigger profit of the combined bank. Another example is if you have a very good distribution network and you are delivering dairy products you can also decide to deliver meat products. The clients you serve are the same so there is no need two trucks to go the retail store. This also should bring some synergies.

Free cash. Perhaps you have a very good profitable business, which makes several million net profit per year. The stage of the industry and the specifics of your business doesn't give you much opportunities for organic growth. Every year you receive several millions and you don't know what to do with them. Just to keep them in the bank for minimum interest rate doesn't make sense. That's why you can use that free cash to acquire some of your competitors since there is no option for an organic growth. Another option is to buy a completely different business which can bring you yield higher than the money can bring you in the bank deposit or from real estate projects. If we are talking that the standard for acquisitions of companies is to buy them at 5-7 times EBITDA then you should expect something around 15-20% annual yield. There is no other investment opportunity which can bring so high yield besides to buy another business.

The motivation of the managers. This effect is much more common for the multinational companies than for the family businesses but it is very strong motivator so let's discuss it. Actually I would say that perhaps it is top three reason for the deals. Every manager wants to manage bigger company because he will have more power, recognition, and last but not least more money. Even if you are a very good manager but you are in charge of a 20 mill company it will be hard to request to have the same salary as somebody who is the CEO of a 500 000 million company. It is a normal human reaction to want to have more power. The fastest way to fulfill your goal is through not organic growth. In other words by buying another company which to integrate to the current business you manage. If you are an entrepreneur the bigger size also does matter but in a little bit different sense. If you have bigger company it will be easier for you to generate more interest from the potential buyers and to receive a better price. One of the most common things which the owners of family businesses in Eastern Europe hear form the fund managers is that their company is too small for their fund. They advise them to do a consolidation and then to call them again to look at the deal.

Tax effect. The effect of that motivation is also more typical for the big multinational companies but it can really have significant impact. What do I mean? If you have a good profitable business you will have to pay some taxes. Usually in the valuation the indicator which is taken is EBITDA. The investor is taking the profit before taxes. If you buy a company which is at a loss then you can use something like a tax credit because with the losses of the acquired company you can deduct it from your EBITDA and from there you will also decrease the taxes which you have to pay. Even if the taxes are low as they are in Bulgaria (10% corporate tax) on 5 mill profit you have to pay 500 000 corporate taxes. I wouldn't say that the tax optimization can be the leading reason to buy another company but it can tilt the scales in one direction or another.

Sometimes the reasons to buy a certain company can be completely irrational but this doesn't matter. Every entrepreneur has his own reasons and he is the person who can decide if it makes sense or not right now to acquire another business.

Once you have taken the decision you have to launch the process and to decide where from you can find the appropriate company for the acquisition. The process when you are buying a company is not that much different than the one when you are selling your business but it is upside down. If I have told you that it will take a lot of time and resources to sell your company have in mind that it will be the same when you are buying a business. Even the expenses for the buyers are bigger because the financial risk is much higher. One of the solution is the investor to put more efforts in order to minimize the risk of making a bad investment. You must be clear that this is not a project which you can execute while you are doing several other things. You have to be prepared to set aside the necessary resources. As in the case of selling your company you can also try to buy a company just relying on yourself and your internal team or you can hire an outside consultant. If you going to buy assets in your local country you can handle the task just with the help of your lawyer. However, if you going to buy a running company and it is abroad I would strongly advise you to use experts' help.

There are two main approaches when you are buying a business. To be the active side or to be on the passive side. In the passive approach the owner of a company has decided to sell his business and he or his consultants might contact you to ask you if you will be interested to acquire the company. Perhaps some of you already have received such requests from friends or from colleagues in your sector. In the passive approach the process can happen much faster and easier but you will be in an unfavorable position compared to the case if you use active approach. Since the seller got in touch with you it is very likely that he will organize an action for his company. This way you will be one of the many investors who would be invited to submit offers for the proposed company. There will be a real auction and you will have competition. This competition will most probably will increase the price of the deal. If there are not many interested investors most probably the proposed company is not so attractive. Even if you end up in a situation of an organized auction you still can reach a good deal but have to be very careful. It is in your interest to turn the process around and you to be the active side in the process.

If you have taken already a decision to buy a company you will be better off to organize yourself an auction and to lead the show. If you take this approach not only you can choose from several prospects as opportunities but also the companies will not be so "polished". Imagine that you want to buy a car. You can either go to the car market and to look at 10 cars within an hour or you can start talking to your friends and neighbors to see if they know somebody who might sell his car if you offer him a good price. On the car market all cars will be "polished" and you can be screwed by buying a car from there since it might have some hidden problems. In the second option you will decrease that risk significantly but you will have to invest a lot more time in the process. You have to choose which approach to use but I would strongly recommend you to be the active part and to choose your car among your neighbors figuratively speaking. Here the M&A consultants can help you because they know where to look for and they will also save you a lot of time. If you are buying a business your focus has to be exactly on that first stage. If you spend enough time and resources on this first stage then you can have a lot of saving down the road with the due diligence process and the integration of the bought company. It is hard to quantify it and perhaps you might end up with the same result as money spend but invest more in the research than in the phase of closing the deal.

If you have decided to be the active side and to organize an auction pretty much you have to repeat the steps which we have discussed so far in the book but this time you will be on the opposite side. You are the buyer.

Valuation of the company

If you going to buy a business then you should use the three major methods which are based on the cash flows of the firm. These are the DCF model, the EBITDA multiplier and the comparison model. It is probable that the owners of the company which you contacted will not have a prepared company valuation. That's why you can help them out in this task by asking them to provide you with a forecast for their sales, investments, and profits. Your M&A consultant can prepare the DCF model for the company, which you are planning to buy. Whatever price you receive from this valuation I hope that I had managed to show you that the price doesn't have to be the only criterion when you decide which company to buy. Pay attention to the structure of the deal, what warranties the owner will give you, and whether you are buying 100% of the company or just a stake in it. All these factors will matter in your decision.

I will be ready to pay higher price if all other elements are lined the way I want. It is like buying a second hand car. It will not be just the initial price. You also need to make insurance, change the oil, perhaps change the tires, etc. All of sudden it can turn out that the actual price is not the 5000 euros you have paid for the car but it is more of 7 000 euros after all additional stuff. You need them in order to be save on the road. If you buy the car from your neighbor you might pay him 6000 euros instead of 5 000 but you won't have to do all this additional expenses after the execution of the deal.

Due diligence stage

Here whatever you do and it doesn't matter how thorough your investigation will be there always be a risk that some problems can show up after the transaction. It is normal to trust a person who has experience in M&A deals and he will be the leading person in the whole process. However, if you are going to buy a business abroad you cannot rely just on that person for the due diligence. Yes, he has the knowledge about the M&A process but there is no way that he will be familiar with the regulations in the country where the company is located. That's why if you going to buy a business in Italy with the help of your M&A consultant you have to hire a local experts which can help you with the due diligence process. Since this is an expensive operation it will be wide before that step to sit down with the seller and to agree on the warranties he is ready to take. First of all you can ask to buy just a part of the company on the first stage and then to have the option to buy the rest stakes. So the deal is executed in several stages. You can also ask to implement an earn-out scheme thanks to which the seller can receive some additional payments in case he reaches the forecasted business plan.

You can also ask some part of the money to be paid in an ESCROW account where they can stay as a buffer for future problems and claims from your side. If the seller agrees to all these demand I would offer him a higher price. Instead of 5 mill euros I would give him 6 mill euros. The idea is that you as a buyer are ready to minimize your risks and you are ready to pay a premium for that pleasure. On the other side if the seller is sure that there are no hidden problems in the company he should be OK to accept all these demands and eventually to receive a better price for his company. If he starts to give you arguments why this cannot happen it is very likely that he is afraid of something and perhaps is hiding something. If this happen then you should be twice more careful in the due diligence stage. If he agrees to your requests then the scope of the due diligence can be decreased which will save you time and money. In the chapter for the due diligence we talked about the major issues you have to pay attention to. In the appendix you also have a due diligence checklist. However, here they are the main critical points one more time:

Delayed payments from the side of the seller about some investments, employee training or the implementation of some software products.All these steps will increase the available cash in the company and will lead to better financial indicators at the moment.

Increasing the deadlines for collecting some receivables from clients. This way some receivable still will be considered good and the company doesn't have to put aside provisions for them or to write them off. The provisions and the write offs will decrease the net profit of the company and no seller wants to do this during an M&A process. If the owner delays the problem then the company will have an asset in its balance sheet which is account receivables. The company will also have a higher net profit because the owner would not do any write offs.

 The seller might have sold one of the major assets such as the administrative building to a third party and take it back on a financial leasing. This way the company will have a lot of cash which the owner would expect to receive and you will have to make payments during the next years for the leasing.

Your consultants and the due diligence team know what to do and they will take care of the process. You as an owner might want to ask some additional questions the seller. His answers can give a lot more insights about the real situation in the company. Stuff which the technical side of the due diligence cannot give you. Here are some of the topics which you should address with the seller:

 Why are you selling?
 What are you planning to do after the transaction?
 What gifts and present the company gives to its clients. In other words what the ethical standards in the company are.
 Do they use any instruments to hedge the foreign currency risk?
 Who are their biggest clients? How long they have been working with them? What part of total sales these clients have and how this proportion changes over the years.
 What do they believe is the image of the company in the society? Their opinion about the subject. Afterwards you can check yourself if it coincide with the public perception.
 What does the owner believe that is the major competitive advantage of the company? Why would he buy his own

company?

Who are their biggest competitors and what are the trends on the market?

How do they acquire their clients?

Who are the three key managers in the company according to the owner and why?

If the financial results of the company are not so great for the last 1-2 years why is that according to the owner?

The list with questions can be endless but the key here is to feel how the business is managed. Is it professionally done and how correct is the owner with his employees. Does he still have the same drive to manage the company as he used to have when he set up the company? If he is not so motivated or perhaps tired this might be a good explanation why the financials of the company deteriorated in the last years.

Financing

Now when you are actually the buyer in the M&A process the financing issue is becoming one of the key topics for you in order to close the transaction. There are several instruments which you can use in order to finance the acquisition:

Personal savings. This is the default approach. Everything comes to the question how much money you have and how big is the deal. Many entrepreneurs tell me that they want to acquire a competitor but they cannot do it because they don't have so much money in the bank. Some of them believe that if the seller wants 5 mill for his company they should have 5 mill cash in their bank accounts and pay the whole price in full right away. This is a normal attitude when you are buying assets but when you buy a business you can negotiate various stages and besides you can buy only a majority stake or even minority stake. Basically you can afford to buy much bigger companies than you think in terms of savings.

Bank financing. In almost cases when you make acquisitions you use some amount of bank financing. For the professional investors like the PE funds it is a mandatory component and very often they use financial leverage to get a better return from their investment. You have to be careful with the amount of debt you use because when you make the calculation most probably the economic outlook is positive and your forecast looks realistic. There is a chance that you can take the bank loan but the business goes down for objective and subjective reasons and then the cash flow you generate won't be enough to make your payments for the principal and for the interest rates. The bank also don't want to get to the situation where you won't be able to make your payments and they have some internal limitations for the amount of debt which your company cam have. It might varies in the countries and for some bank groups but as a general benchmark you can use that the debt shouldn't be more than 3.5 times the company EBITDA on an annual base. Here an important factor will be if the company which you are buying has a profitable business. If this is the case then its cash flow can be added to the cash flow of your company.

You will increase the total EBITDA and you can receive more money from the bank to finance the acquisition. Have in mind that most probably you will have to put a pledge on both companies in favor of the bank. If you are making an acquisition abroad you have to decide which bank can finance the acquisition. No bank in the foreign countries will know you and you don't have relationship with any bank there. At the same time the bank you are working with in your home country might not have branches in the foreign country. The perfect solution will be if your serving bank is an international bank and has a branch in the other country. For example most bank in Bulgaria are foreign owned and for example if you are working with Unicredit bank you will have no problem to do an acquisition in Italy or in the other countries where they have branches. When this is not an option you can try a local bank but then it will take more time for them to investigate your company and decide if it will worth the risk. Therefore you just have to forecast that during the negotiations and be careful what you put as deadlines in the term sheet.

It can turns out that you cannot provide the necessary financing during the period which you have received to close the deal. The most embarrassing situation is everything to be ready and agreed on and not to be able to sign the final contract because you couldn't secure the financing for the deal.

Seller financing. This is not so popular form in Eastern Europe and in Europe as a whole but it is common in the USA for example. Seller financing doesn't mean that the seller will give you the money for the transaction but it is more that he will be ready to reschedule the payments during the years. This way you can pay the whole amount through the cash flow which you will generate in the next 1-2 years from the business which you acquired. For example the price is 10 mill euros and you have to transfer him 6 mill euros. The rest 4 mill euros you have to pay him during the next two years and you can generate the money from the cash flow from your main business or even from the cash flow of the acquired company. Yes, this is not the best option for the seller but this way he can receive a premium in the price and it also depends how many option he has for interested buyers. If there is no line of investors the seller either should agree on a seller financing or not to have a deal at all. If you based in Eastern Europe I doubt that the seller will agree but you can check in the beginning of the negotiation process if he is ready to consider such option.

Bonds. This is already one of more exotic options for the family type of business but the big corporation very often issue corporate bonds and use the proceeds to make acquisitions. Here I would also add and the mezzanine financing which we discussed in the various types of buyers. If you are a risk taker and the bank doesn't give you anymore financing then you can also use mezzanine to bridge the shortage in the financing amount.

Selling an asset and get it back in a financial leasing. It is not a typical instrument but if you have come across a great investment opportunity and don't have enough cash right now you can agree with a leasing company to sell them your administrative building and to rent it back. This way you can secure more free cash and in 3-4 years when you have more cash you can buy back the asset.

Integration of the Business

Here you will experience your biggest problems especially if it is your first acquisition. We talked in the previous chapter how important it is to help the buyer for the transition period. Now all these troubles will be on your head in full extend. Here are some advices which you can follow when you make the integration of the acquired company:

Your main priority has to be to try not to pay the whole amount in full at the closing. Either you can bind some of the payments with the financial results in the next 1-2 years, the famous earn-out scheme or you can try to use seller financing and to pay in several installments. This as a step is as important as all the rest advices down the sheet.

Start the process of integration before the deal is closed officially. If you have signed the term sheet and now the auditors are doing the due diligence you can use the time to learn more about the culture of the company. You can use instruments like Trello and Slack to see how the employees communicate inside the organization. What problems they have, what motivates them? How they see their future in the company? etc. You can get together the executives of both companies and to talk about the future plans of the company. Of course this depends on the agreement of the current owner and most probably he won't be very happy to do it before the deal is secured on 100%. In general it will be in your interest to pull in advance this stage as earlier as possible.

Be completely straightforward and honest with the employees about your plans for the future. Nothing is more confusing than the uncertainty. As a friend of mine says: "the second best answer in a sale is No"

You can request a meeting with the HR manager. If they have done some surveys of the employees you can analyze the data and see what the main issues in the company are.

You have to find the hidden leaders in the company and perhaps you can make them official. They will become your biggest allies in the integration process if you manage to win their support.

Let the changes happen gradually. Don't be in a rush to make all changes in the first 3-4 months. You still are not so familiar with the culture of the acquired company and how the processes work and you will take a risk that something will backfire in your face.

The first 30 days after the deal is signed are the most crucial ones and that's why it will be good if you are present psychically at the premises of the acquired company. You will be able to observe the first reactions from the first raw. That's why it is important that you have built a corporate structure in your current business so that you can have the luxury to leave it to operate by itself for some period of time. If you are present in the first 30-60 days in the premises of the acquired company the employees will see that you are dedicated to this deal and you are trying to make it work. It is not just a financial operation for you as sometimes is the case with the financial investors. Besides nobody can replace the effect of what you have seen and heard with your own eyes and ears.

When you have a clash of two completely different cultures there is no such thing as an excessive communication. It doesn't matter how many times you announced that you will not fire people or shut down the factory, or make significant changes. It will be OK to communicate it one more time. Use difference channels and various messages but keep assuring the employees that the change of the ownership will be only for the good of the company and their own good.

At the end of the chapter I want to finish with a couple more important issues in regards to the acquisition of another business. One of them is when the most appropriate time to acquire another company is. First of all you have to be ready for that step but in general the best time to buy a business is when nobody else is buying. For example everybody is scared because of some economic uncertainty or some turmoil which is going on. For example as it is now the situation with the Covid and all the fear and uncertainty in the business circles. Exactly in this moment you can find diamonds in the mud and you can acquire them at prices for which you can just dream about before the Covid situation. Of course you should have stable business with stable cash flows so that you are not in financial difficulties but as you know the economy works in cycles. Even if at the moment the outlook is very gloomy be sure that in 2-3 years most probably things will change and all stakeholders in the economy will be much more optimistic. If you managed to buy a company which worked very well before the financial crisis and now objective reasons got it in difficult situation then it is very likely that you will get sunshine again on your street after the storm. The entrepreneurs and the bank without strong nerves will be scared and they will be ready to sell you the business at a very good price during the storm. That's why I believe that the best moment to buy a company is during a financial crisis.

You don't have to forget that sometimes not closing a deal is actually the best deal which you can make. You have invested a lot of time and money in the research of a company, have done due diligence but still something in your gut tells you that there is something wrong and doesn't give you a piece. This sixth sense very rarely lies to you and when we are talking for a process of mergers and acquisitions which is more of an art than science there is nothing wrong to base your final decision based on your gut feeling than on any quantitate indicators. You have to accept the spend time and money as a gained experience. Next time the time which you will need to get to this stage of the deal will be a lot less and most probably you will spend a lot less money. That's why these 100 000 euros spend on the research of this opportunity can leave it as a sunk cost or just to add them to the cost for the next deal. And most of all the lack of enough cash in the bank doesn't have to stop you to research a specific investment opportunity.

You can even agree to buy just a mimority stake in the target with the option to buy the majority stake in some period of time. This way you will decrease your financial risk and you can direct your attention to much bigger companies in size. The smaller a company you buy the more dependable it is on its owner and the harder the process of integration will be. So don't worry to have big appetite. There are enough instruments and mechanism which can allow you to acquire a company which is bigger in size than your current business.

What should I do with the money

You have closed the deal successfully and managed to receive all or almost payments for the transaction. Now all of a sudden you will have a new problem. What should you do with the money? This can be a small amount if your business was not so big or it was not very profitable but we can also talk for several million euros. Most people probably will say: "I'd like to have the rich peoples' problems". Actually according to the statistics around 70% of the people who won a lot of money form the lottery have lost it within several years. This fact proves that maniging the money which you have made through the sale of your business won't be an easy task. Because of that there are people or companies which main activities is actually to manage other people's money. In 2002 when I was in the USA I worked with a team of six financial consultants from Merrill Lynch which managed a portfolio of 800 million dollars.

Unlike most lucky guys who have won from the lottery the probability that you will lose your money is very small. The reason is that you know how much time and efforts it cost you to develop the business which you have just sold. That's why you will be very careful with the management of the proceeds from the sale. These money didn't fall from the sky and you didn't win the lottery. On the other side because you are an entrepreneur and you mind is programmed to work like that it will be hard for you just to leave the money in the bank. You know that money which stays in the bank in general doesn't bring income and this thought will bother you. After some rest you will start wondering what to do with these money.

Decisions that have to be made

The first step after the transaction is closed is to take some rest. Long years of managing your business and the whole process of selling the company which can sometimes be very stressful made you exhausted for sure. I am sure that even if I asked you right after the deal you would tell me that you didn't want to run any business anymore. Just want to sit on the beach and play cards. This feeling will pass by. If this stage will take 2 months or 2 years I cannot say. It is individual thing. Nevertheless the exact period you will need some time to recharge your batteries. Just enjoy that period.

You have to realize the new situation. In practice you are not richer than you were before the deal. The only difference is that your assets are now more liquid. Before the deal you had a business which was valued at 10 million euros and now you have 10 mill euros cash in the bank account. So you are as rich as you used to be. Now the issues which will make you worry will be different. You won't worry anymore if the truck has broken and you cannot deliver the goods. Instead you will worry if the bank in which you keep your money will go bankrupt or if the investment you made with the money will be profitable. Only a person who has been in that situation can imagine that these can be real problems. You can ask a friend who had saving in banks which got bankrupt. In Bulgaria we recently had a bank which went bankrupt.

You have to decide if you will deal personally with managing your money or you will hire a professional personal banker or a company.

You have to communicate with your family the new situation and what your plans are. Now they will have a lot of expectations from you. Perhaps your kids will expect to receive some of the money. You friends will ask you for small loans and favors. There is no right answer but whatever you have decide it will be good to communicate it clearly so there is no wrong expectations. The expectations can be in the base of some family conflicts.

You have to sit down with a tax expert and see what taxes you have to pay actually on the proceeds from the deal. It might turns out that a huge part of the money in the bank are not yours.

Perhaps it is time to write your will if you don't have one or to set up a trust fund for your kids.

You can think about the opportunity to leave some of the money for charity. You can set up a foundation or to support an existing foundation. If it will be related to health, education or other cause is your personal decision.

Now if you have closed a bigger deal and received more money you will have more opportunities. It will be hard to spend all money. When I have talked to entrepreneurs I have always wondered why they are so stubborn on the valuation when they sell their company. If they receive 10 mill or 12 million in both cases neither they or their kids will be starving. However, very often for a difference of 1-2 mill the whole deal can fail. In general the statistics reveal that very few people have the financial knowledge and can manage their personal assets well. How many of the people you know have personal budgets. While I was doing my MBA in the USA a professor who was teaching "wealth management" class told us that only one out of seven people in the world is a generic saver. The other six people whatever amount of money you give them they will spend all of them.

Back then as a poor student with a scholarship of 15 000 dollars I was thinking that if I make 40 000$ annually I will wonder how to spend the money. At the same time in my class there were people who were making 70-80 000 dollars per year and they had less savings than I did. The good news is that you as an entrepreneur most probably learned how to manage your finances and most probably you will be one of the seven people which the professor called "generic savers". After you deduct the taxes which you have to pay for the transaction you have to make yourself a personal budget. You have to calculate how much money you will spend per month for living expenses. You have to see if you will have some other revenue sources. After that you can decide what amount of the money you can invest in such way that it will not have a huge impact on your lifestyle if you lose that money. It will be wise before you come up with ideas for the investments to put aside 15-20% of the money in an emergency fund.

As a result you will have an investment budget and now you have to decide if you will do this personally or you will give the money to somebody else to manage them. If you decide to give your money to a third person to manage you will have two options. In the first case you can have a financial consultant who can provide you a full service. That type were the financial consultants I worked with at Merrill Lynch. As a first step you would have to fill some questionnaires in order to find out what is your tolerance to risk. i.e. how risky you are as an investor. This depends of course on your preferences but also on how old you are, you family status and many other factors. After the consultants determine what your investment profile is then the money will be divided in several groups and it will be invested in several assets which have different level of risk. For example it can be shares, bonds, and even cash deposits.

For that pleasure, somebody to do the whole work and to manage your portfolio of investment, usually the financial consultant will charge a annual management fee of 1% of the assets he manages. He will really take care very well of you. You will be pampered. He will call you for your birthday. He will remind you and congratulate you for family events, etc. The other option is to the same exercise with a company which will not provide you such full service. They will also give you a test to determine your risk profile. Very often this will happen online. They will do the initial division of the money into group assets and from there on it will be your responsibility to follow the investment and to decide if you have to rebalance your portfolio. There will be nobody to pamper you and to congratulate you for the graduation of your daughter. Since you will not receive that personal attention the annual fee which you have to pay for the management of your asset can be just 0.2% of the assets. Yes, the bigger part of your investments will be in index funds and they will not be managed actively but very often the index funds beat in yield the funds which are managed actively by the portfolio managers.

If you decide to manage your assets by yourself this will turn into a full time job for you. Perhaps you don't believe me but you will see how much time it will take you to do it. I even recall for a deal where an entrepreneur sold his company to a foreign investor but had to help them with the transition for one year. Formally he was part of the board of directors but he was so busy with the management of his money that the foreign investor complained that he actually doesn't spend enough time to help them with the transition of the ownership. However, if you decide to go down this path (to manage the money by yourself) lets discuss some opportunities for investments.

Type of investments

Everybody has some preferences to the various classes of investments but the best decision is what Warren Buffet says: "Don't put all your eggs in one basket."

Real estate. This is a traditional instrument for all people in Eastern Europe and not only there. That's why most entrepreneurs put a significant part of their saving into real estate assets. Actually there is no need to sell your business to see that actually most people put their saving into real estate. Eventually the logic is that the house, which you bought will not need anything in order to exist and will not disappear in 5 years. The reality is that not always people make money out of the real state because the prices can also go down and can have maintenance expenses. Yes, if you look at the data in the log-term perspective the prices go up but you can invest in a period of 3-4 years when actually the prices go down. Besides the increase in the price of the assets the other option to make money out of the real estate is from the rent. Actually this has to be your leading indicator because the other thing is pure speculation and nobody can tell you how long and how much the prices will go up. With the yield from rent is not so easy in some countries. It is not so high in Bulgaria because the rents are not very high and most of the apartments are empty in Bulgaria. If you put the taxes, the expenses for maintenance and the operational expense you might find out that it might not make sense to have 5 apartments which are empty. The reason is that in poor countries like Bulgaria the income of the people is not high and they cannot afford high rents. Plus the population is declining each year and you have fewer people which could rent the apartments. On the other side in markets like London, Paris, Istanbul the situation is very different so it depends on the country in which you are. For example in

2008 we had a peak of the real estate prices in Bulgaria.

Then the financial crisis came and the prices went down with 40%. Now in 2021 the prices already exceeded those in 2008 but I think this is just a speculation. For these 13 years the population of Bulgarian decreased with over 600 000 people (according to the National statistics the population decreases every year with 50 000 people) and most probably at least 100 000 new apartments were built. In the first year in the university business majors study about supply and demand and the crossing point of the two lines. If the demand is decreasing and the supply is increasing where you do think the two lines should cross? In countries like Bulgaria a huge part of the investments in real estate is speculative and that's why most of the apartments are empty. There are not enough people. Yes, the apartment building cannot go bankrupt like a bank but you still can have an earthquake and to lose everything.

Hotels. This is an option which is very close to the real estate for most entrepreneurs. Since you are tired you don't want actively to develop another business. In this case a hotel looks like a good business which doesn't require a lot of efforts and can bring you some income. It turns out that actually it is not so easy to make money out of a hotel and it is a specific business. If you cannot reach some occupancy rate then most probably you will lose money from the operation of the hotel. The good point is that you can look at the hotel as some type of a safe place for your money so that they don't stay in the bank and to take a risk with its bankruptcy.

Renewable energy. Here I put the solar and the wind parks. This is also an investment which doesn't require you active participation. It is very popular in Bulgaria. Here you are dependable on the regulation and at what level the government will buy the electricity from you. This way the yield which you have forecasted in your business plan when you were making the investments can go down significantly. In the EU we have regulations which makes the government to buy the electricity from the renewable sources at higher, not market prices, and that's why you never know when that policy can change.

Agricultural land. This is perhaps one of the most secured investments. A lot of people decided to invest in land which led to increase in the prices of the agricultural land. As a result the yield from its rent when down. However, despite what the yield is it is a safe place for your money.

Stocks. Here we will go to the other extreme as a level of risk compared to the agricultural land. Yes, historically you can see that the investments in stocks can bring you 10-11% on an annual base but you must have long-term horizon and a patience. Most people, including myself, believe that they are very good and they can "beat" the market. At the end of this game usually the small fishes are those which are losing their money. That's how on one side in the long run you should make good money on the stock exchange and at the same time a lot of people have lost a lot of money on it. Even if you think that you understand from financial indicators and financial reports I would recommend you to invest in index funds which just follow the trends in the market. It will be very hard for you to beat the market. If the professional portfolio managers who are doing this for living in most cases cannot beat the market why do you think that you will do it. Always there are some exceptions from the rule but it is more likely to lose and that's why you will be better off with index funds. The index fund is the perfect tool for any newcomer on the stock exchange markets.

Gold and other precious metals. Here the risk is much smaller than with the stocks and that's why it will be good to have in your portfolio of assets some gold in case world crisis happens like now with the Covid-19.

Another business. Right after the deal this option will look absurd to you but with the time you will start thinking again for such option. You will have the option to be an active side in the process of buying and developing a new business or to be a passive player. If you want to be the active side and the new business is in the same sector as your previous company you have to check if you have signed a non-compete agreement. What is the scope of that agreement and for how long it is valid. You can deiced to start a company in a completely new industry for you. I mentioned in the beginning of the book of the owners of one companies which we sold, which had three different types of companies and they sold all of them. So you might become a serial entrepreneur. You can also be a passive investor in other businesses. Something like a personal investment fund. In this case you must have a prepared management team which will manage the company on operating level or the companies which you buy to have such team in place. If you do that option you can come back to the level of stress which you had while you run your previous company but it can also be a little bit different. That will be if you don't invest all your money in the business but just half of it. This way you know that you have secured your pension. This business won't be exactly a hobby but even if it fails you won't feel so stressed as with your previous company.

Invest in startups. A little but different option of the above one is to invest in startups. This is a long topic. I personally had one startup and now I am developing a second startup project. If you are really interested in the topic you can look for my other book which is about how to set up and develop a startup. Here the investments are very high risk because according to the statistics around 90% of all startups fail. In regards to that I would say that this type of investment is even riskier than investing on the stock exchange. On the other side if the startup project is successful the money which you can make from it can even exceeds the money which you have made form your business which you have developed for 20 years and have sold for several million dollars because of the high risk the correct approach is to invest in several startups simultaneously. On this early stage of development of the startup projects nobody can say for sure which project will success and which one will not make it.

The only indicator which can differ your investment from the casino is to invest in teams which you know. This way you know that they will do their best in order to succeed and you also know they will not take your money and go to the Hawaii to spend them. In other words to deceive you intentionally. Of course it will be also good if you believe personally in the idea, which the founders are trying to develop. In most cases when you invest in startup project you will make initial investment of 50-100K dollars per startup. You will also be named a business angel. An additional advantage if you decide to invest in startups is that you can follow the development of the new technologies and trends form the first raw. You will work with young people who wants to conquer the world. Startup investments are risky asset and that's why at the moment you make the investment you must write it off completely from your mind. This way you will be prepared for the probable outcome from the investment. Don't forget though that the market at moment implies that such startup can be sold for at least 10 mill dollars in 4-5 years. Such money you won't be able to make with your traditional business even after 10-15 years of efforts.

Last but not least as an option is to decide to give your money or at least a part of it to your kids. This way they can develop their own businesses. You as a parent will decide when and how this can happen because you don't want them to have everything for granted. I might be almost 100% convinced that you as an entrepreneur will not waste your money but I cannot be sure for your kids since they would receive the money as a gift. You can also can decide to set up a trust fund but this is not so much an investment option.

The key at this stage is to enjoy completely the moment of the successful deal and to understand that after you feel ready for action again you will have a new challenge in front of you. How to manage your money. I have almost never met an entrepreneur who after the sale of his business kept all the money in the bank and just sit on the beach and drank cocktails. You will get to some moment where you have to actively manage your assets and this is some type of work after all.

Last Advice

During the last years you have seen a lot of articles and comments how the level of merger and acquisition deals is on record levels. The reason for that record levels are mainly two. The first one is the huge amount of money which were printed by the ECB and the FED after the financial crisis of 2008 and the second one is the limited opportunities for organic growth of the companies. This way the only option for the managers to grow their business was to make acquisitions. This trend also impacts and smaller countries like Bulgaria. Here the deals are a lot smaller and we didn't have access to much of the printed money. That's why the deals which happen in Eastern Europe differ a little bit from the big deals which you read about in Forbes and in Bloomberg. Despite the record levels of M&A deals still only 10% of all deals are closed successfully.

A person can ask himself why the success rate of closing deals is so low. You have read this book with advice and now you should be able to handle one M&A process successfully for your business. Actually there are many books on the topic of company acquisitions. This is not a new topic which hasnot been discussed and researched before. Despite all these prerequisites something must not be the way it should be if the success rate is so low. The problem with the low success rate for closing M&A transaction is that this is a wasted resources of the top executives and their time is very valuable. Let's get into more details on the major factors which makes the success rate for closing M&A deals very low in most markets:

Your company is unsellable. We talked that a business can be sold when it is in good financial condition and making profits. It doesn't matter how profitable was your business last year. It can get into hardships and this can be due to objective or subjective reasons. Then the owner of the business will be pressed to the wall and he starts looking around for investors who can buy his company and save him from bankruptcy. The bad news is that in this situation nobody will want to acquire your company or the price they will offer will not please you. That's why waiting too long and taking the chance the business to become unsellable is the major reason why the company cannot find an investor and to close a deal.

Unrealistic expectations for the price of the company. When for many years you have woke up and went to bed with the thought of your company it is normal that you are not anymore objective about its real value. At the same time the investor who for some reasons wants to acquire your company is looking at your company with a lot more pragmatic view. That's why if you want him to pay you 100 euros and in the neighboring country he can acquire a similar company for 90 euros you can guess what his decision will be.

"I am feeling I am selling my child". This is a pure psychological moment which can be overcome only by the owners themselves. No M&A consultant can help you with this internal battle. The owners who have several businesses take this decision much easier because they know that this is just a business. For those of you if this is your only company which you have built for 20-30 years it will be very hard to decide to sell.

"My business - that's me". With this factor we have a psychological barrier too. After many years in that daily routine a person can ask himself: "What will I do tomorrow morning when my company is sold?" The only solution to solve this problem is to find yourself a replacement. You can find it in spending more time with your family. Just imagine how many times you neglected your wife and kids while you were dedicated 24/7 to your business. It can be also some type of hobby which can take most of your time and of course you can start another business.

"I am still having fun". If a company owner still fells pleasure from what he is doing every day there is no power on Earth which can make him to sell his business. Unless he receives a huge bag with money, of course. Sometimes you need a very big bag. The expression that "when you are having fun at work this means you don't work" applies in full extend here.

Fear or Greed. These are two human qualities which are the reasons for most financial misfortunes of people. It doesn't matter how often the history repeats itself people still don't learn their lesson. The stock exchange market is a very good example for that.

"I am the smartest person in the room". In most cases when you negotiate with a big foreign investor they have send some managers which negotiate the terms with you. When a person has created a very successful business from scratch and now he is courted by the big companies it is normal his ego to grow up to the roof. This will show very clearly when the hard moments in the negotiations arise. At that point an attitude which can be described with the words "some managers which are on a pay check will tell me how to run my company" will not help for the successful closing of the transaction.

MBO and MBI deals

There is one big reason which has a huge impact on the number of the bought companies. It is related to the often discussed topic in the book for the corporate structure of the companies. If I have to summarize for the last time then the lack of an established corporate structure in a company prevents your business from growth and it also decreases the chances that you can sell your company. How exactly it affects the number of closed deals? As I mentioned in the beginning of the book one of the main reasons why an owner wants to sell his company is because he is tired. This is the result of 20 years of everyday efforts and you also don't have a prepared person to whom you can leave your company to be managed. In Western Europe very often you have family businesses which are managed by professional manager and the owners are just shareholders in the companies. I have noticed that some company owners are trying to implement that practice in Bulgaria but in reality it doesn't work out so well. They hire a CEO but actually the CEO rarely is the real manager of the company. Here I have into account the case where the company owner has only one business. When you have several companies then you as an owner are forced to delegate the management to managers because you have no other choice to run all the business by yourself.

Yes, those CEOs are formally the top managers but in reality they act more as operating managers. Their real task is to help the owner with the operating problems because he cannot handle all the work since the business grew significantly. That's how in practice these CEOs almost never take strategic decisions about the business. When the moment the owner to retire comes it turns out that he has nobody to trust completely and he is forced to sell his business. On the other side I have a lot of friends which are good managers and have ambitions to run big companies but they never really get the chance to do it. Since we still have a lot of opportunities in Bulgaria most of these young managers decide to grab an opportunity and to start their own business instead of to manage a big company. I understand the company owners that it is not so easy to "entrust their child" to a stranger and he can ruin. If the owners cannot get over this fear they won't have a prepared manager and when the time to retire comes the only option left is to sell the company. There is a lot of psychology in the behavior of the entrepreneurs but there are also objective reasons why they cannot trust completely their managers. For example they cannot determine which of their managers have the qualities to really manage the company as it is their own business. When the owners are making their choice they emphasize mainly on the technical skills and they are the least important in this situation. If the company owner owns a dairy company he believes that if the manager didn't work as an executive at another dairy company or at least in a FMCG firm he won't be able to handle the job.

For them it doesn't matter that this manager might have had a lot of professional achievements. This perception also grows down the hierarchy of the company and is applied to the lower organizational levels. I remember 2003 when I came back from the USA. I had an MBA with a full scholarship from an American University. Besides I had two years experience as a consultant at the Small Business Development Center and a MBA internship at Merrill Lynch. Despite all these credentials I couldn't find a job in a bank in Bulgaria because I didn't have bank experience. I wanted to work in the field of investment banking (mergers and acquisitions) but because at that point there was no such department in the banks in Bulgaria I applied for positions in the corporate credits department. Since I didn't have the experience nobody wanted to hire me. At the end I started in a small bank. Every reasonable guy just need a couple of months to see how things are operating in a bank and what he is supposed to do. It is no brainer. After 6-7 months I had no problem to switch the banks and to have a better paid position in a bigger bank. I already had a formal bank experience. That's why I believe that the company owners doesn't have to concentrate so much on the specific experience and on the technical skills but to pay more attention to the soft skills of the managers. I will give an easy trick how you can find out if the manager is ready to run your company as his own business. Let assume that right now he is receiving around 10 000 euros monthly salary.

Since this is his current pay he would want to pay him similar salary and bonuses and you find it for completely normal. However with that salary he will be OK to keep his living standard and whether he will receive the bonuses or not it will not be so crucial for him. He will act more or less as a high paid employee. In this situation I would offer him a monthly salary of 4000-5000 euros. Of course the numbers are depending on the country where you are based. With that level of compensation he won't be starving. The idea is to see if he will be ready to sacrify some of his current living standard for the opportunity to make a lot of money. That's what any company owner does. You start a business and you know it will be hard in the beginning but you can become very successful. You want him to behave like you. That's why the bonuses he can receive should be unlimited. For example the bonus can be 20% of the net profit of the company. You can even increase the percentage if the profit goes above some levels. With this scheme it might turns out that this year his compensation can reach 1-2 mill euros. Many company owners will object here: "How come the CEO will receive 1-2 mill euros? He is just an employee. I have created that business and have taken all the risks". Yes, you are right but if you think along that line you will never find a manager who will act and behave as an owner. You don't have to forget that every manager who is taking a pay cut of 50% for the upside potential of the bonuses actually feels confident in his skills and in practice thinks as an entrepreneur. It is a completely different topic that you don't have to interfere into his work.

If you remember the football analogy I gave you a couple chapters ago. You cannot expect and judge a person based on his results when you have sold his two best players. From my experience with the entrepreneurs in Bulgaria this is a very common case. As a result we have the following paradox. On one side company owners who complain that they cannot find decent managers who can run their businesses as entrepreneurs and on the other side we have young professionals who complain that the local company owners act as craftsmen and want to control everything in the companies they are supposed to manage. There is no problem with that situation and it works well. However you won't be able to find people who can take over the operating work form you and you have to be forced to sell the business when you got tired. Now I can tell you as an example the case when in 2010 I was an Interim CEO for 4 months of the biggest Bulgarian plastics pipe manufacturer. I mentioned earlier that in 2009-2010 the company already had financial difficulties and together with German experts we had to restructure it. When the Germans couldn't agree on the terms with the owner I took over the management of the company in the beginning of March. The idea was within 4-5 month to restructure the company and to prepare it for a sale. At that time I was 33-34 years old and I couldn't make a difference between a PVC and PPP pipe. Despite that for a very short period I got to know the business, increased the sales with 20% and decreased the net loss with 25% for the last quarter compared it the previous quarter.

I also found an investor who was ready to pay 1 mill euros for the company and to take over all liabilities. Now when I am thinking about it I am wondering how the owner trusted me to do the whole operation. Perhaps the reason was that he was in Turkey and he had several companies so couldn't manage the company by himself. As you can see things can work out successfully. Besides the pure psychological moment the owner also must establish a corporate structure in the business. That's where we started this topic. If it is lacking in the company it will be hard for any manager to take over because everything in the company will be related to the owner. One of the solution is if the owner decides to take this step and appoints a new CEO to go literally to the jungle for 5-6 months. This way his employees will not have access to him and they have to work with the new CEO.

The described situation in significant reason why in the family businesses we don't see so many MBO and MBI deals. These are deals which are done by inside or outside managers and supported by financial players. In order to have such deals you must have real active managers in the company. Not just people who do the operating tasks.

A key part of the established corporate structure of the firm is to have a real and active board of directors. The board of directors is one of the most important bodies in the company but its importance is neglected in most family business. All big companies have such structure because the regulations require it but in practice it doesn't perform the functions it is supposed to do. Usually people from the operating management are appointed in the board or even worse. It can be just friends of the owner so that he has formally such structure. It is not a coincidence that there is a requirement in the big company at least one of the board members to be an independent member. Here are the six major benefits of having a real active board of directors:

The independent members have different points of view on the problems which the company has to cope with. This is normal since they are not part of the operating management and are not influenced by the inside policies in the company

They have experience and know-how form other industries they have worked at. It is very likely that in these companies they have already handled the problems which your business didn't handle yet.

These people have a network of contacts which is completely different than the one of the operating managers. This network can be used for the future development of the company.

They will have new and weird questions. The discussion of these questions can bring another perspective and all of sudden to receive the A-ha moment which you need to solve a problem. Not knowing the company in details thy can ask question with the curiosity of a kid which can make the operating management to say: "Xm I haven't thought about this from this angle".

It will be nice if in any board at least one member is not an industry experts but has contacts with various companies and their business processes. For example business or strategy consultants. These people have encountered so many different cases that they can provide interesting analogies with other companies.

The independent members can also add value with their specific knowledge. It can be in the field of finance, marketing, PR, data security but this is also of a value. Besides their business experience they are also an experts in a certain field.

The idea of the independent members in the board of directors is to bring this new perspective or as it is called "fresh eyes" which can be lost when a person is involved in the everyday work. There are two options how you can build such board:

A board which has more of a consulting character and where the owner will take the decision by himself. The good point is that he will take them at least after a heated discussion.

In the second option the members have a real vote and you can get to the case where the members accept a decision which is not supported by the majority owner but hey: "isn't that democracy? A good example is the dismissal of Steve Jobs as a CEO from Apple. Whichever option you choose the benefits of having an active board of directors comprised of independent members are obvious.

Another option which you as an owner have so that you don't have to sell your company is to leave the business to your family. We talked that they might not have the desire or to have the necessary skills to manage the company. It is a tough decision but have in mind that this is common problem all over the world. Despite the fact that this option looks very attractive to any owner only 30% of the company in the world are passed over to a second family generation and only 12% of the companies actually are in the third family generation. The majority of the family companies are either sold to or managed by professional managers. On one side the lack of good managers leads to more deals on the market. At least many companies are out there for sale. At the same time this also prevents most deal to be closed. Now I see a new trend in Bulgaria and I think in the whole Eastern Europe. There are good companies which are for sale and we also have people who have free cash and don't know what to do with it. At the same time when I am talking with them and offer them to buy a certain good company they are not sure for that because they don't have the time to manage another business. If these people had prepared managers then they will jump right away on these opportunities because they are really good companies. Otherwise I cannot explain myself how come somebody might reject the opportunity to buy a company with increasing sales, no debt and to pay only 5 times its profit. At the same time these entrepreneurs are wondering what to do with their free cash and looking for investment opportunities.

Turnaround businesses

Sometimes your company can get into trouble and it financial results to worsen. Perhaps you got into a fierce competition with the multinational competitors or you just got tired and don't put the same energy in the business. It doesn't matter. In this situation the owner starts wondering what to do with the business and how to sell it when it is generating only loses. It is much harder task than the case when you have a profitable company but there is a saying in Bulgaria which says that there are passengers for each train. What can be the reasons that somebody will want to buy your company although it got into trouble? The first one can be for tax saving. Just this one won't be enough for a deal to be executed but it can convince the buyer that it make sense for him. It can have a huge effect on his taxes and that's why he might be ready to give several millions for the company although it is losing money. Another reasons can be that the current problems of your company can be just temporary. There are enough prerequisites that your business can generate again good profits in 2-3 years.

Here the investor have to investigate very carefully what were the reasons which led to the current financial problems and to prepare a DCF model. Since the DCF is oriented to the future it might turns out that the company still has some value. If the investor uses the multiplier of EBITDA or compare it to other companies from the sector it might turns out that the value of your business is one euro but it might not be exactly true. Actually if you are in such situation you don't have to be obliged to sell it.

You can just give it to specialized experts in turnaround consulting which can try to restructure it for you. The fact that today it looks like that your business has zero value might not be like this in three years.

Lately we have many companies which are sold for a lot of money although they are not profitable or even in some cases they don't even have much revenues. Of course this applies mainly for technology companies and startups. I can give you an example with world giants like Uber which keeps on accumulating losses but despite that it is valued at over 60 billion dollars.

Even Whatsapp was bought by Facebook for 19 billion and they barely had any revenues. In these cases the principles for the valuation are completely different than the ones for the traditional business. I am not sure how sustainable is this model for valuing startups but as log there are investors who are ready to pay that amount of money this is Ok for the owners of startups. So, basically you can have a company which is at a loss or with minimal revenues and still to sell it for good money. In this case you have to offer something else to the investor. Usually this is the client base. By default all these technology startups should have a huge growth in the number of their clients/users. The idea is that one day this huge client base will start to bring them more revenues and the company will become profitable. This principle can be even applied at the bigger more traditional business. Imagine a big company which is operating at a loss with the idea to gain a market share and later on to turn it into profits. I can recall right away a couple food retail chains in Bulgaria and I am sure that you also can come up with similar examples.

So if you have a startup you still can sell it for a good price although its financials are nightmare.

Another case for acquiring a not profitable business is when the company directly cannot get break even from its main activities but indirectly it can bring other benefits to the investor. A good example here are the media. Most media hardly make money nowadays when the free content is a default case in internet. However the media also bring tools for influence which can benefit the owner. That's why we witness that there is a significant interest from the investors to buy various media despite they are not making so much money. Another good example in this group are the football teams. I am sure you can give examples in your home country and also world famous case such as PSG from France. The most emblematic case is the Chelsea and Roman Abramovich. This guy became world famous thanks to its investment in Chelsea.

Sometimes some companies cannot be saved and the most normal thing is to disappear. The reason can be objective like a change in the regulations or the development of the technologies. It can also be a subjective reasons like the unprofessional management of the company by its owner. This is actually the more common reason. In this case you usually sell out some of the assets and whatever is left over goes to the creditors and the tax authorities. Unfortunately in countries like Bulgaria we don't have the practice to search responsibility from the owners for the bankruptcy of the companies and that's why we don't have deals for 1 euro in Bulgaria.

Here I mean when the owner is a local entrepreneur. In this case if you are the investor you can make a very good deal by buying some assets and leave the rest to the owner. If we have a situation where a big multinational company got into financial trouble they cannot do the same thing. They also have a huge reputational risk and they have to be very careful about it. Therefore in this cases you can buy a company for one euro which has a potential to be restructured. I can give you an example with the French food retailer Carfour. They had operations in Bulgaria. It was not directly from the HQ but it was done through a franchise with a Greek company.

The Greeks operated the food retail stores in Bulgaria under the brand of Carfour. The business got into trouble and they had to declare bankruptcy and got out of business. For the regular clients the impression was that Carfour got bankrupt in Bulgaria which was not the real case but this is what matters to the clients. This is a huge reputational risk and I am sure that the French guys are not happy at all with this situation in Bulgaria but cannot do much about it now. That's why if you are investor I would advise you to check which foreign companies are not doing so well in your home country and to contact them. You have a very good chance to buy their business for a good price. Why this didn't happen with Carfour I cannot say. The point is that I tried to show you several cases which allows you still to get a good price for your business although it is not very profitable. So you still can make money out of it.

Last Advice

At the end of the book I want to go over some issues which I missed to discuss in the book or they are so important that it worth the time to go over them again:

When the potential investors come to your premises pay attention if they have printed in advance the information memorandum which you had sent and whether they have taken some notes on it. If they have done it this means they have a serious interest in your company. They are not fishing and have prepared for the meeting. If they didn't do it is very likely they just want to research the competition.

When you are buying a business don't be arrogant with the seller. Sometimes his company might not be in the perfect financial condition because he has made some mistakes. This doesn't give you the right to behave like a smart ass and to tell him that you know all the causes of all problems and you can fix them. Even if from outside it looks perfectly clear that the problems are due to bad marketing or distribution perhaps the situation is not that simple. Eventually nobody knows the business better than his current owner.

In regards to that you have to be respectful to the expectations of the seller. We had cases where clients have good companies and they want us to find them an investor. In general we tell them that under this conditions we can find them an investor who can pay 7-8 times EBITDA for their business but this valuation looks very small to them. In several months I go back to the same guys and this time I offer them to buy another business which is also as profitable as their company and the owner is ready to sell it for 5 times EBITDA. Surprisingly after log negotiations these guys offer the owner to pay him 4 times EBITDA. At that moment I asked them: "Why do you want 9-10 times EBITDA for your company and at the same time you offer only four times to the owner of the company which has the same profitability like your business. If this is fair offer I can organize the other owner to buy your company for 5 times EBITDA You actually should have a premium since you believe that 4 times is fair value" The answer is that it is different because the business are different.

I realize that each company is different but what is the big difference. Eventually it doesn't matter if you produce salami or electronics the main goal of any business is how much money it generates. A friend of mine who was a partner in several companies with 4-5 other shareholders told me that they have the following rule which they follow strictly. When you want to buy their stakes in the business you make them an offer to buy your stake at a certain price. However, the other shareholders have the right if they believe that the price is undervalued to buy your stake at the same price you offered them. This way you are inclined to offer your partners a fair value when you want to buy their stakes. I am not saying that when you are a buyer you have to be generous and not to protect your financial interest but you also have to respect the other side in the deal. It doesn't look fair when you have two identical business to ask for 8 times EBITDA for your company and at the same time to offer only four time for your competitor.

If a company is making very good profits there is something fishy in the whole thing. Either the niche in which the company operates is still small and new and the big players didn't find out about it or the financial reports might not be representative. If we put aside the practice to fix the financial reports sometimes we have companies which have found a very good niche and are making good profits. There is nothing bad in that but you have to be clear that these level of profitability will not be sustainable in the long run. This is important when you are preparing the DCF model for the valuation. The world is a very competitive place and there are a lot of very smart people. It won't take long time before the entrepreneurs finds out about this segment and they will switch to this niche since the opportunities for profits there are above the normal market levels. I want to say that in the longer period of time the markets are efficient and that's why be careful not pay for profits which won't be there in 3-4 years.

If you are selling your company, you are not prepared for the process and don't have enough resources it is very important to communicate with the buyer why it takes so long time for some of your steps in the process. The investors will request a lot of information from you which by default you should be able to give within couple of days. You won't be able to do it and will feel embarrassed. That's why you will keep silence and this can be perceived completely in the wrong direction. That's why it is important to manage the expectations of the buyer in the process.

Don't underestimate the time which you need to close an M&A deal. It is unlikely that it will happen for else than 6 months and in general be prepared for 12 months.

If you insist the whole price to be paid to you in a lump sum in cash it is very likely that this will cause some doubts in the head of the investor. He will think that there are some hidden problems and that's why you are in such a hurry to leave the company as soon as possible. If this is not the case it will be wise to explain the buyer why you insist to receive the whole amount right now in cash.

It is also important how you will structure the remuneration of you M&A consultant. It is clear that the main goal is to close the deal successfully and for that he should receive the lion's share of the remuneration. However for you it is also important not to close the deal at any cost. Sometimes it is better to have no deal at all than to have a bad deal. The M&A process takes a long time and your consultant invests a lot of resources. If you structure your contract in such way that he will have a financial interest only if the deal is signed then don't be surprised if he intentionally or unintentionally kind of "force" you in to that direction. He will try to convince you that the deal is awesome and you have to sign it. Therefore think about a way how you can align your interest with his interest.

It is very important to have a written business plan. Especially if you are selling only a stake in the company to a financial investor. Yes, the financial reports are important but any investor is interested to know what will happen with the company after he invest in it. That's why if you prepare a short business plan with forecast for the next 3-4 years it will be of great help to you in the process. It will also serve as the base for the preparation for the DCF valuation later on. A lot of family business owners don't have such written business plan because everything is in their head but there is no way how the buyer can read what is going on in your head.

When the process is going to the end and it looks like that the deal will be closed successfully it is important to make sure that the buyer has the necessary financing for the transaction. If he start thinking about this now there is a risk that he won't be able to secure the money and can ruin the deal and also the whole process with the other interested buyers. It is a delicate topic but it will be good if you can check in advance. In my practice we had such example when the buyer couldn't come up with the money because from the time of the term sheet to the payment the currency of his home country deprecated 30%.

Don't hide problems or information which is clear that will show up later in the process. The problem here is more with the trust than with the specific info. Most people start any negotiations or relationship with trust. At the moment they feel that the other side is hiding something from them or is lying then they will put every information or step under suspicion. This will make the whole process and the negotiations hard to execute. You have to be 100% sure that the other party won't find out about the hidden info in order to play that game.

When you are the buyer in the deal be careful not to get in touch with any clients, suppliers or employees of the seller without his consent. If you put yourself in his shoes you will understand why. It is normal that you would like to gather as much info from various sources but everything must have some limits.

In regards to that you must be very careful with the confidentiality agreement you have signed. In some countries like Bulgaria it the parties might neglect this documents for the lack of real consequences but if you do in in Germany or in the USA the court there might have a different view. Even the fact the court case will be in a foreign countries implies that you will have huge legal expenses.

When there are several shareholders in the company it is normal that one of them will be more motivated to sell and other might not be so sure about it. Before you start the whole M&A process it will be good if you have a written agreement what you have agreed on and on what price you will be ready to sell. The process takes time. There will be a lot of heated discussion and problems to overcome and it is normal that at some point one of the shareholders to back off and to give up from selling his stake. The whole deal can be jeopardized. The investor will wonder what strange company it is where the owner doesn't know what they want. That's why it will be good your oral agreement to be put into writing.

A main factor for the success or failure of a deal is how committed is the owner to the M&A process. If he is doing it just an experiment to see what is going to happen then the chance nothing to happen is extremely high

You have to be very careful with the CEOs of the companies. Depending on the case if you are the buyer or the seller their role is different but in general not always their interest will be aligned with that of the company owner. They have no guarantee that if the investor buys the company they will keep their job. They might try to break the deal by providing not complete or misleading information to the investor with the idea to keep the status quo. If you are the buyer they can mislead you again by describing a bad picture so that you decide not to buy the company.

Sometimes the sellers don't act very cooperative in the process. Since they were approached by the investor they think they run the show. They are not ready to negotiate any of the disputable questions because they didn't invite the investor. My approach is that each opportunity worth to be researched carefully because you don't know from where you can hit the jackpot.

Nevertheless if your business is developing very well at the moment or it has financial difficulties don't forget that it will not always be like that. That's why be open to any opportunity and don't wait the time when you will be pressed to take the first offer on the table

The longer an M&A process takes to close a deal the bigger the chance that the deal will not close at all. You cannot expect to complete it in 2 months but if a 12 months pass by and you are not close to the end a red light should show up that most probably it will not happen at all. There is a term "deal fatigue" which explains it very well.

It is important not to forget the operating tasks around the business. As we talked about 90% of the talks don't complete with a signed deal so it is important to take care of your business during the whole process. You don't want to wake up in the situation that there is no deal and a significant part of your profit disappeared because you were too busy to pay attention to your clients.

Franchise business. It is a long topic which we didn't discuss in the book but sometimes it happens that you buy or sell a franchise business. Here besides the agreements between the seller and the buyer you also have to take into account the opinion and the requirements of the franchisor. Without his consent you cannot have a deal. Besides with that type of business you have to decide if it is worth to buy a franchise business at the first place. The question is whether you will have to pay a fee and to receive just a book with written rules or you will receive real help to handle your problems. If it is just for the rules you can get the same effect by buying a book about the topic for 10 euros, similar to that book, and you don't need a franchise contract. My point is that you have to decide very carefully if it will worth money to have a franchise business or you can set up an independent business.

However, for some people who don't have much business experience this might be a good option for ready business.

 Don't assume that a deal is done by signing the preliminary contract or the so called term sheet. I gave you several examples where things got wrong at the stages after the term sheet. That's why until you receive all your payments you have to be on top of your toes.
This book will not make you experts in mergers and acquisitions and this is not its goal. I wrote it with the idea to give you some basic knowledge about such process and its steps. Most of you will encounter that problem only once in your life. You cannot rely just on your personal experience and I hope that this practical guide will help you to be more prepared for the moment when you have to sell or buy a company.

List of Contributors

First Author Kaloian Kirilov is an entrepreneur with 20 years of experience. He completed his MBA with full scholarship from GVSU, USA, where he worked for the Small Business development center (SBDC) and also for Merrill Lynch.

Secon Author Professor Sanjay rout is an CEO of Innovation Solution Lab, He had worked more than 15+ years in innovation,Research and Knowledge Management.He had author of 100+ books on Futuristic topics.

Editor Professor Prangyan Biswal is the Director of IL Publications,wh is an eminent Researcher & Educationist.

Notes

ISL PUBLICATIONS

ISL Publications is a global Research Development, Publication, Advisory, Think-tank, Policy Research, Innovation Development, Business Consulting, Communication, and Advisory Firm working on Future Business Solutions.

www.ingramcontent.com/pod-product-compliance
Lightning Source LLC
LaVergne TN
LVHW040029190726

843490LV00014B/1428